Sane Singing

A GUIDE TO VOCAL PROGRESS

D. Brian Lee

Better Baggage Publishing

ISBN 978-0-9997774-8-0
Library of Congress Control Number: 2018905547

First Printing, 2018

Better Baggage Publishing
Potomac, Maryland USA

www.betterbaggagepublishing.com

Acknowledgements

Justin Petersen, teacher, scholar, friend—I thank you for the many chats, deep thoughts, and reading recommendations over the years. You are the best study buddy!

My colleagues at the Speakeasy Cooperative have been a great sounding board and cheer squad.

My students and the followers of my blog and videos—thank you for telling me how I can serve.

Christin Coffee Rondeau, my editor-angel. Thank you for your skills, your encouragement, and for making me a better writer.

I am grateful for my voice teachers—Mary Walkley, David Christopher, George Gibson, and David Jones—who have taught me so much about singing, sanity, and kindness.

Harry Fox, my brilliant, wise, and super-supportive partner—you gave excellent editorial advice and helped me stay on track, over and over and then some. Your talent for talking people off the ledge is legendary. I am ever grateful.

Contents

1. First Things

The Motive

The industry built around training and advising singers is a massive mound of discombobulation. There are hundreds of "methods" and "programs" and thousands of teachers, schools, courses, and seminars—some good, some bad, and some too weird for classification. How can we make sense of it? Where do we start?

Voice instruction is largely done as one-to-one tutoring, hidden from public view. It is often called "private lessons" for this reason. With no true licensure for voice teachers and huge variation in teaching styles and methods, it can be very difficult to find the training you need. A singer may study with the same teacher for years and not know whether their training is anything like anyone else's, or even whether it's any good. This creates challenges for the student, who can lose valuable time in the wrong learning environment, with nothing to compare it to.

This book is about self-advocacy—taking control of the course of your vocal life. I share my discoveries along with plenty of opinions, warnings, and encouragement. It's about figuring out what you need and how to get it!

Lace up your boots! It's a long, winding, fascinating trail.

—D. Brian Lee

Modi Operandi

❖ You are a singer if you sing. It doesn't matter how well or badly, whether you get paid for it, which genre you sing, or for whom you sing. In this book, all singers are equal.

❖ I am a clumsy dancer around the peculiarities of English pronouns. Therefore, I will sometimes use the plural forms "they" and "their" even when referring to one person.

❖ I use the Oxford comma and commas outside of quotation marks with a clear conscience. I have learned that this is considered "British style".

❖ I use the terms "exercise" and "vocalise" interchangeably for vocal patterns that are designed for practicing.

❖ If something seems bizarre or stupid, it either is, or it needs to be restated better. If I've written something that doesn't make sense, and I'm still alive, feel free to ask me for clarification.

❖ This book was organized with a logical sequence but, being a collection of essays, should be readable or skippable in any order.

My Peculiar Path

Most future voice teachers receive encouragement for their singing at a young age. They take voice lessons through their teen years, sing lead roles in the school musicals, apply to college or conservatory voice programs, and graduate with either a vocal performance or music education degree. They take courses in diction in several languages, sing in choirs and opera scenes, and get frequent coaching from pianists and music directors who help them learn their music. Many go on for a master's degree in voice.

Not me! My musical and educational path went to a lot of unusual places. I have studied and performed professionally as a singer and on the piano, flute, double bass, saxophone, and viola. I have taught all of those instruments, plus a few more, both privately and in faculty positions. I constantly take deep dives into old books and recordings, leading to delightful discoveries. The results of my sleuthing have led to hundreds of blog posts and countless lively discussions.

My broad experience with performing and teaching, plus a burning curiosity for independent scholarship, probably would not have blossomed if I had gone through the usual academic track of getting a voice degree. Clearly, I don't fit well in boxes, and I have never wanted to. All of this has made me a better teacher.

I grew up in a tiny town called Churdan (pronounced "sure DAN") in the state of Iowa, in the United States. In high school, I was into all things musical, which included bands and choirs every day, musicals (as chorus member, lighting director, orchestra pit pianist), and plays. During my school years, I had lessons on trumpet, French horn, piano, and oboe, and taught myself flute, alto saxophone, tuba, clarinet, and euphonium. I yearned to pick up the double bass, but that didn't happen until 11 years after high school.

In my last year of high school, I had the opportunity to take about a dozen private voice lessons from Mr. Robert Reck, the high school choral director in nearby Scranton. He was kind and sensible, kept things simple and did no harm, and I improved. I enjoyed voice lessons—for all too short a time.

I started college as an oboe major with a performance scholarship. I also auditioned for a university choir. The director warmed me up through a three octave G scale and said, "You have talent; you should take voice lessons!" The department assigned me to the studio of the faculty soprano. Unfortunately, my singing abilities took a tumble—I became self-conscious, tight, and inhibited. I sang "Amarilli", a famous baroque Italian aria, on my first and last singing exam in front of all the faculty, and it did not go well. Humiliated, I quit singing, judging that I had a bad voice and no talent for it. I did not sing again for an audience for 20 years.

Fortunately, I was having success as a woodwinds player and pianist. I won a concerto competition as an oboist during my freshman year, and won two more concerto competitions as a flutist by age 21. I paid my way through college as a pianist for singers, instrumentalists, and ballet classes, and learned a lot of art song and opera repertoire that way, while keeping my ashamed singing mouth shut. During my second year of college, I switched from oboe to flute as my major instrument—a significant change of direction, but far from the last.

Even after two degrees in flute performance, it didn't occur to me that perhaps some *teachers* could actually be bad. When studying flute, oboe, and piano, I felt like every teacher had helped me grow in some way. One almost never hears of a flutist being "ruined" by a bad teacher, but you hear that statement rather often with singers. I wouldn't say that I was *ruined* vocally, but I was definitely *stunted* by poor teaching.

Beginning in my undergraduate days, I taught private lessons on woodwinds and helped singers learn their music from the piano ("repertoire coaching"). I enjoyed giving lessons and coaching very much, and my clients improved, so I was doing more right than wrong, most of the time. After getting my flute degree, I took summer classes in the Suzuki Method for flute, violin, and double bass. The Suzuki Method, also called Talent Education, has a lot of good things to teach all teachers of young people, regardless of the subject. The "one point lesson", "ear before eye", the "learning triangle" of teacher, child, and parent, and how to work with people of all ages, were all hugely helpful in my teaching, including working with singers.

Right after my bachelor's degree, I took a six-month course in tuning and repairing pianos. Piano tuning helped hugely with listening skills in the voice studio, including intonation, hearing specific harmonics, and how pitch and timbre are perceived. After piano tech school, I took four years off from coursework before going for a graduate degree, unless you count a mixology course, which has been quite useful in nonmusical ways.

Between degrees, I studied with two superb and famous flute teachers, Thomas Nyfenger and Bernard Goldberg, who prepared me well for grad school. Mr. Nyfenger's words and touching, unique flute playing still ring in my head at times. I remember him saying at a master class in Maine, "You all have a place in music." It was a rare and welcome word of encouragement. I felt that he was right, but I also was coming to realize that playing in a flute section in an orchestra might not be the right career goal for me.

Earning my bachelor's degree in flute at the University of Iowa had been a difficult and stressful experience. At Iowa, I learned a lot about politics, egos, nepotism, and grit. The flute faculty there were not encouraging, perhaps because I had switched from oboe to flute, which annoyed them. Yet outside of school, I was winning competitions and playing concerts. While struggling with my fluting, I continued to gain valuable experience (and dollars) as a pianist for voice studios and ballet classes, and as a collaborator in recitals.

Seven years after my bachelor's degree, I received a master's degree in flute performance at Bowling Green State University. I had a teaching assistantship and performed four recitals, although only one was required. The two years at BGSU felt like a proper completion of my basic flute training, which previously had been so spotty and unfulfilling. Judith Bentley, my flute professor and advisor, was a gifted and creative teacher. The experience of intense study and performing many challenging works as the flutist for the New Music Ensemble was good for my musical soul. I also came to understand that although I definitely had a talent for teaching, going for a tenure-track professorship was no longer a glamorous goal.

Soon after my master's degree, I attended the University of Maryland to add a public school teaching certificate to my qualifications. My justification was that a public school teaching job would be a way to have a stable career in music. I tried voice lessons again, to be better prepared in case I had to lead a school chorus, and this time, the lessons were not a disaster, but they seemed to reaffirm my lack of vocal talent. However, I was starting to understand some of the issues that make teaching singing such a tricky business compared to instruments. During those Maryland years, I dated a member of the graduate opera program and got a closer look at the strange and sometimes neurotic world of the pre-professional singer.

Since singing was still not happening for me, I decided to take double bass lessons in order to boost my resume for the orchestral side of public school music teaching. Being tall with strong hands, I was well-suited to it and I enjoyed it a lot. I advanced quickly and was able to get jobs in union orchestras and play sonatas and concerti in recitals after about three years of study. I still sometimes miss the bass; it was a relatively fun chapter in my classical career.

My public school teaching career lasted five years, and it was hard! I was often exhausted and had little energy for my own music. I also moved from Maryland to Florida during that time, eventually settling in St. Petersburg. One year in a middle school in Florida was the horrendous finish to my public school teaching career. I have incredible respect for the hardy souls who make a career running school music programs. It was definitely not for me.

On the bright side, one of my school districts paid for the bulk of a second master's degree which I did part-time while teaching. By the time I quit public schools, the degree count was four:

- Bachelor of Music, flute performance
- Master of Music, flute performance and pedagogy
- Bachelor of Science, music education
- Master of Arts, instructional design

That may have been two degrees too many, but I learned *something* with each of them.

After leaving the schools, I began working in the information technology field, which became a good financial basis while continuing to figure out music (and everything else) in my life. Living and working in St. Petersburg was pleasant, but I was restless. I had sold my bass for much-needed cash. I returned to the flute for a while and played in orchestral and chamber music groups but wasn't feeling the musical love. At least I was still enjoying teaching private lessons on various instruments.

In my continuing attempt to try to get more musical merriment back into my life, I started viola lessons. I even commissioned a beautiful hand-made viola. This led to some juicy experiences playing orchestral masterpieces such as Respighi's *The Pines of Rome* and the Sibelius *Violin Concerto*. There is an amazing auditory sensuality about being inside a large orchestra, playing magnificent music. However, there is also the issue of being a soldier in an army under the strict command of a conductor, with little opportunity for personal expression. One day, while playing my viola in the pit orchestra for a run of *Peter Pan,* I looked up at the stage, then down at my fellow musicians honking and sawing away, and said to myself, "I'd rather be up there!"

My search for a voice teacher who could help me with my musical theatre experiment led me to the marvelous and bubbly Mary Walkley. Her main clientele consisted of performers in professional musical theatre and popular music. She taught with clear sequences of exercises that had explicit purposes, and I improved! I had not experienced such organization and results with my two previous teachers.

Mary's emphasis was on getting "the mix", the smooth coordination between low and high pitches with no discernible break or crack in the voice. Her approach did not use imagery much and referred back to fundamentals frequently, as opposed to slowly revealing an infinite library of secrets to learn. The fundamental exercises were always a place from which one could go even further.

Using musical theatre as my point of re-entry into singing worked very well and bypassed a lot of my baggage from previous "classical" training. I began to know my voice much better and to understand that there was such a thing as vocal training that uses empirical, logical principles rather than magical catch-phrases. While working with Mary, I successfully auditioned for musicals, where I had some intense learning experiences and social adventures. This is when I began studying books about singing, starting with those influenced by Seth Riggs, who was one of Mary's teachers. I also became more conversant in vocal anatomy and acoustics.

With Mary, the voice teacher curse was finally lifted! No longer did I feel like a hopeless case. Working with a good teacher and understanding my voice better gave me more clear ideas about what to look for in a teacher or training system. After nine years in Florida, I moved back to the Washington DC area, my previous home territory.

Soon after the move back to Maryland, I started getting paid singing jobs, mainly as a substitute tenor in the many professional church choirs in the area, or for special music for holiday services. Singing in many places with many conductors and having to learn music quickly in order to lead a tenor section was great training for me. I learned that it wasn't so important how perfectly beautiful a voice is, compared to well how it can serve the music and bring people together.

I had just started teaching voice lessons at the end of my time in Florida. This became a much bigger part of my life after my return to Maryland. I came to feel that teaching voice is much more interesting than teaching instruments. Voices are unique; they are used in every imaginable genre; they have tangible and intangible elements to master, and there are words—so many fascinating treatments of words! I found that I had a knack for helping all kinds of people to sing better and eventually stopped teaching instruments.

I was getting used to being considered a voice teacher, but that didn't mean that I was stopping voice lessons myself. After getting settled back in the DC area, I started to look around for a teacher. I was looking for someone special I could click with at that stage in my vocal life. After a few months, I succeeded, although it involved two hours' travel each way—not so local.

In the early days of the internet, voice teachers who had been more or less isolated began to communicate with each other more. This lead to musical kingdoms and gospels colliding, with lots of wild arguments, but it was also a great springboard for learning. I became aware of many teachers, books, and historical pedagogies for the first time. One of my early online connections was with Katherine Posner, a teacher and soprano who had studied for many years with Cornelius Reid. Reid wrote several important books on vocal pedagogy (how to teach singing) between 1950 and 1992. Katherine's descriptions of the approach to singing that she studied and taught were compelling. I read Reid's *The Free Voice* and was fascinated, so I devoured all of his other books, including *Bel Canto, Psyche and Soma, Essays on the Nature of Singing,* and the *Dictionary of Vocal Terminology*.

Reid's books and concepts were radically different from how I had been taught in the past. For example, Reid eschewed "placement", the idea that the voice can be projected to or from a focused location in the body. He concerned himself mostly with the fundamental laryngeal functions of the voice, which were to be discovered and improved through spontaneous responses to targeted exercises. "Freedom" is a favorite word of his. Feeling fairly certain that I needed more "freedom" in my singing, I asked Katherine to help me find a teacher. She gave me a list of Reid-trained teachers which led me to David Christopher, based in Wilmington. David had been an assistant teacher for Reid in New York City. I contacted him, and he graciously agreed to teach me.

I studied with David for four years. He was a successful and kind teacher, and generous with his time, eager to convey Reid's functional approach to a less experienced voice teacher. I started to sing a lot more classical solo material while studying with him, but we almost never worked on repertoire in lessons. Lessons consisted of 30 to 60 minutes of exercises, but the exercises were much more musical than those I had encountered before. I learned an immense amount about singing as I discovered how a carefully selected musical stimulus can move a voice toward better functioning. There was a strong element of improvisation in many of the exercises.

With David, I learned about basic vocal functions as the basis of learning to sing, which I group like this:

- the *messa di voce*, the ability to grow and diminish on a single note, leading to better legato and sustained phrasing
- the trill, including runs and other agile movements of notes
- the staccato, including onset, accent, and rhythmic action in vocalization

He stressed that they all need to be present and available at any moment for optimal singing. I learned a lot about how to exercise and hear these vocal functions. Aside from his technical expertise, David had a knack for keeping the student comfortable and open to whatever was coming next. Observing his teaching was always fascinating and yielded many notes for future study.

During the time I was working with David on vocal coordination and freedom, I was working with a repertoire coach in Washington, DC. Gillian Cookson was a fabulous support as I explored repertoire. Her piano and language skills were astounding, and our work was delightful. In addition to helping me with how to perform repertoire, her finely tuned ears helped me to identify technical issues to work on and take back to my teacher.

The next teacher was George Gibson. I first met him at one of his master classes in Washington, DC. One of the scheduled singers canceled, and I volunteered to sing in his place. It was a very positive experience, and I learned that George came to DC monthly from Arizona to teach a lot of the local singers, so I asked to begin working with him right away.

George taught me how to form vowels that would work with classical repertoire. As strange it may seem, I really needed that. George liked to include repertoire in the lessons, and with that, I learned much about making a physical connection to the text. He helped me to work through (most of) my phobia about singing in German, and he helped me with French and English as well. Working with text became less mysterious for this former instrumentalist.

While he was not fond of a lot of imagery, George did have ideas about breath and resonance that were more mainstream than those that my previous teacher taught. This played with my head a bit, since a few of his concepts were similar to the "magic words" that I had failed to grasp in college. However, after studying with several teachers and some years of teaching voice, I was increasingly able to translate between previous and current training. It became easier to know when something new was introduced, as opposed to an old idea with new words. Often in retrospect I have seen that I *needed* to hear old ideas with new words!

George also helped me to get out of my own way when performing. I loosened up quite a bit and took more risks. Although I was a high tenor, I think I waited almost three years before bringing in an aria with a high C. When he liked it, I was over the moon! We worked on arias from *The Pearlfishers* and *Faust* and lots of Mozart and Handel, as well as many art songs. His advice was so sensible and solid. He did not hesitate to remind me of basics over and over.

Eventually, as George was winding down his Washington studio and preparing to retire, I took a break from lessons for about two years and continued to study many books. I kept my eyes open for a new teacher but was not in a hurry.

I applied for a summer course for teachers, but it was overbooked, so at the last minute, I signed up for "The David Jones Teacher Mentoring Program" in New York City. I had read David Jones's online articles for years and was strongly encouraged by some friends to check out his teaching in person. I was skeptical, having been crestfallen many times when attending master classes. I was delighted to find his teaching inspiring, deep, and highly effective in the diagnosis and solution of vocal challenges. He also had an unusually strong sense of responsibility to attribute his exercises to their sources (teachers and colleagues), never even hinting that he alone was the Messiah of singing.

In addition to an incredible command of how to work with high and low, heavy and light, robust and recovering voices, David stressed the way in which a teacher conducts himself. Respect and kindness were always present, both in the master classes and in private lessons. Lessons with David were about in-depth diagnosis and specific exercises to remedy faults and build strength and flexibility. I found new richness and stability in my voice with David and am forever grateful. As of the time of this writing, I still sing for him regularly and I always learn something new.

These teachers each had a wealth of knowledge. I certainly did not learn everything they know, but after several years with one teacher, it was sometimes helpful to get a new point of view, new words, and a new training regimen. Working with a new teacher has usually helped me to understand the previous ones better.

Like every other voice student, I interpreted what my teachers were teaching through my own filters and ability to understand. I doubt that we singers ever internalize 100 percent of what our teachers are saying in the exact manner that they meant it. My teachers might be appalled to read what I remember from my work with them! That is a natural consequence of the tradition of one-one-one study.

It was during my "George years" that I started my blog, *Vocalability.com*. The continuous research yielding cross-connections among old and new texts, discussions with colleagues, and giving and taking lessons kept me brimming with ideas to work out in my writing.

I must mention my beautiful relationship with books! Many fantastic old texts about singing have been forgotten, and many famous ones are misrepresented as people quote people who quoted people who quoted people. My deepest book-learning has come from reading "primary source" materials such as those listed in the bibliographies of dissertations and textbooks. There is no substitute for going to source documents and forming your own conclusions (and questions).

In the Appendix, I have an example of one of my deep dives, with my translation of Francesco Lamperti's landmark debut of the word *appoggio* (the infamous "support" in English). While working on that project, I saw that translations and interpretations of the term have wandered over time, leading to our modern confusion about the term.

It was both sad and satisfying to read works by authors such as David C. Taylor, Franklyn Kelsey, and Herbert Witherspoon from a century ago and realize that they are still relevant regarding how vocal pedagogy has veered from an empirical approach of "cultivation" to a mechanical, atomic approach to "production" and a worship of all kinds of science related to the voice.

My dear colleague Justin Petersen has guided me to many of these wonderful resources old and new, for which I am very grateful. We have spent many evenings discussing books and ideas in great depth. We pored over such authors as Frederick Husler & Yvonne Rodd-Marling, Peter Harrison, Edward Foreman, Cornelius Reid, Theodore Dimon, and Herbert Witherspoon, who go deep into both the philosophy and practice of learning how to sing. I've included some excerpts that inspired me to study all of these writers in "Authors Who Pushed Me" in the Appendix.

It seems probable that my adventures with flute, oboe, piano, voice, saxophone, double bass, and viola all had something to do with looking for the voice I lost at age 19. The decades of coaching and teaching singers, singing and playing in all kinds of ensembles and theater pits, working in schools and private studios, the struggles with my own voice, plus large endowments of curiosity and patience, have all aided my teaching. I used to regret all of my detours and sidebars, but no more. They make me the teacher I am.

Sharing independent research and writing projects with peers and students is much easier now than it was just two decades ago. This allows everyone to participate more in the collective body of knowledge. My blog and this book are part of that. My goal is to encourage more sanity, logic, humanity, and art in voice training, all of which can be obscured in this age of hyper-abundant information.

The Two Big Questions

In early 2017, I conducted the "Vocal Satisfaction Survey" which received over 300 responses from singers of many genres, locations, and levels of achievement. As an independent voice teacher and researcher, I did not intend to make this an academic project, but rather an informal and practical set of 22 questions to get people talking about their training and vocal happiness. It worked! The most detailed and interesting responses tended to come from the following two questions, and helped to focus the writing of this book:

What do you think is the most difficult part of voice training?

What do you wish you could have improved about your voice training?

Looking ahead, these questions merge into one big one:

> *What do I need to know when seeking and evaluating vocal training—things to pursue, and things to beware of?*

Here we go!

2. Training

Why Bother?

Why do you want to train your voice? The answer to this question will be very important for your lifelong vocal journey. It will be the reason you keep on after setbacks. There isn't one right answer, but here are some common ones, good and bad:

- To rid yourself of bad habits.
- To liberate your unique voice.
- To enjoy singing more.
- To become rich and famous.
- To have a better shot at a career.
- To build specific skills, like the ability to sing for a long time without tiring, to increase range, and to be able to ornament or riff.
- To please people.
- To prove the naysayers wrong.
- To increase self-esteem.
- To maintain your voice as you age.

The motivation to improve needs to come from inside of you. If your love of singing and/or leading others in song are your leading motivations, then you will probably enjoy training more than someone who is motivated by ego or popularity. If you are not yet comfortable with your own voice, know that you can always improve it. Learning how to sing well is one of the greatest joys in life and is always worth it!

Do not listen to ignoramuses who say that you either have a voice or you don't, so don't bother training. Yes, some people sound amazing even before training, but many very successful singers did not amaze listeners in their early careers. They worked on their singing and improved it, just like other great artists and athletes.

The athletics analogy is especially good for singers. We train for the same reason athletes train—to reach toward excellence, to keep our bodies in the best fitness possible, and to compete when necessary. Like athletes, sometimes we need to check in and re-train, even after going pro. Our bodies change over time, habits and physical conditions come and go, and the repertoire we sing may change at various stages of our lives, depending on how our careers and personal growth proceed.

People vary a lot in how often they need to work with a voice teacher, especially after their student years. Some professionals take a lesson every week, and some skip years. In Part 4 of this book, where I explain the Self-Assessment Protocol for Singers (SAPS), I will give detailed, easy-to-follow ideas about how to get some perspective on your own singing abilities over time.

Your Team

Professionals in every field usually need a team in order to excel. For singers, this might include a voice teacher, one or more repertoire coaches, a singer-friendly throat doctor, and perhaps other professionals who are not directly related to singing, such as bodyworkers, nonmusical coaches, counselors, friends, and family. Some you will need for specific expertise related to singing, while others help you with general well-being.

Singers who do not have professional aspirations may also have a team of helpers, or they may need only a voice teacher. Whether pro or not, the voice teacher is by far the most important part of the team for the developing singer. A majority of the great singers you may admire maintain a relationship with a voice teacher occasionally for their whole careers.

It is unlikely you will have the same team for a lifetime, although some may be with you for many years. As your needs change, your team members may need to change. Sometimes there is a shorter need for a coach with a certain specialty, for example, or a very good teacher seems to be saying the same things to you all the time, and either you or they need to change. No blame— sometimes it's just time for one or both of you to move on. Oftentimes, a new point of view leads to new growth.

Talk with peers about their teams. Who do they like? What was the experience of working with them like? What are their strengths and weaknesses? Explaining your goals and asking singers, "Who would you suggest I work with?" is a great conversation starter. Most people will be eager to give you an opinion. In the arts, there is no substitute for people talking with people about their people! You will usually get your best leads this way.

Teacher or Coach?

Voice Teacher: A professional who works with singers to train their vocal fitness, including healthy vocal and general bodily function, mental conditioning, and training for flexibility and endurance. Another term for this is "technical training". Voice training is learning how to sing better in general.

Vocal Coach: A professional who works with singers to help them to prepare repertoire for performance, including repertoire selection, style, interpretation, and diction.

I have heard a teacher say, "In my opinion, the 'technician' and 'coach' distinctions wouldn't even exist in a perfect world." While there is overlap, the distinction between voice teacher (vocal trainer or technician) and coach (rep, style, musical issues) is important and needed. The purview of both is vast, so it is not surprising that one would specialize in either of these functions.

Some professionals are skilled in both technical teaching and coaching, but they are not "better" than the specialists. However, when specialists come together, the result can be stronger than if everyone is a generalist. For singers who are assembling their "team", knowing the skillset of potential teachers or coaches is important so that they can address their particular needs as effectively as possible.

It's important to note that in many parts of the music industry, "vocal coach" now means "voice teacher". The evolving terms mean that you need to verify that the person you hire is offering the services you need. Ask them whether they teach vocal technique, repertoire, or both. What they actually do is a lot more important than how they label themselves. Excellent teachers of vocal technique seem to be harder to find than performance coaches at the time of this writing.

Finding a Qualified Teacher

Anyone can call himself a voice teacher. There is no licensure or legal regulation of the voice teaching profession. There are various private-label certifications, as well as vocal pedagogy certificates issued by post-secondary schools. Some of these certifications can be earned in as little as nine days while others take years. A person can get a degree in "voice pedagogy" (also called "vocal pedagogy"), but unlike public school teaching or speech therapy, there is no government-regulated license or industry-wide continuing education or testing required.

This "Wild West" situation means that a private teacher without a degree may be an excellent voice teacher, and too many people with doctorate degrees in voice are terrible teachers. You have to be an educated advocate for yourself and do some research in order to get into a good studio, and then you need to be aware of how to evaluate your progress.

Two prime qualifications to look for in a teacher are teaching experience and a record of teaching students who sing well. A teacher's performing career will naturally inform their teaching, but a star performer isn't automatically a star teacher. A lot of universities and conservatories hire artist teachers who are winding down major performance careers. Often those teachers bring excellent and useful performance coaching skills (see previous essay "Teacher or Coach") but offer little help for training the voice itself. Some of these artist teachers learn to be good voice teachers over time and some don't.

It's good to investigate as much as you can in advance, asking current and former students how they feel about their progress and about the teacher's teaching style. Look at the clientele of the teacher. Do they seem to have success with people at your stage of development? Schedule a lesson to figure out whether the teacher is going to be someone you can work with. No teacher, no matter how successful, is the right one for everybody.

Everyone appreciates a nurturing and kind teacher. Singers vary a lot in whether they like some degree of pushy or critical traits in a teacher's style. Personally, I find that a very experienced and knowledgeable teacher who knows how to guide me in a kind and positive way is ideal. I prefer to be encouraged more than pushed, most of the time. I like to be informed of "areas for improvement and how we will get there" in a cordial manner.

I personally don't care much about the teacher's voice type. My teachers have consisted of two baritones, three sopranos, and a tenor, ranging from horrible to excellent.

As for how the lesson goes, look for a teacher who doesn't fill the time with stories and small talk. I like both exercises and songs—as a teacher and mature singer wanting to stay in shape, heavy on the exercises! The vocal training part of a lesson can be compared to personal training in a gym. I want to work on the athleticism and bodily fitness of singing under the guidance of someone who can help me find better form and function, but always with a musical mind.

If all the students of a teacher sound similar, step away! If many students of the teacher sing well and sound unique, that is a good sign.

Remember that when you go to a teacher for the first time, you are auditioning them as much as the other way around. Ask a lot of questions and keep a list of your questions in writing, so that you can ask the same questions of different teachers and start to understand similarities and differences.

Don't fuss about a *perfect* fit. The point is to find someone you can learn and grow with. As you become more advanced and experienced, you will know better and better what you want in a future teacher. Combine your personal impressions with rational criteria for comparison. Personalities are important, and someone who your friend doesn't like might be fine for you. If you have done your homework and have taken a sample lesson, you can make a well-informed decision about this important member of your singing team.

Dealing with a Bad Fit

Personalities of teachers vary hugely on the spectrums of effective to ineffective, nice to mean, and pedantic to creative. It can take a while to find one who is effective, kind, fair, creative, and nurturing. If you study with more than one teacher, you will soon discover how unique each teacher is, unless they are thoroughly trained by one of the certified methods out there and are purists within that method. It is likely that you will get a stinker at some point!

If you are an advanced singer, the problem is not so dire, because sometimes there is some small thing or two that you can take away and use and forget the rest, and you will have a sense of when to move on. If you are newer to voice study, it's harder, but you can still assess whether things are working or not. How would you answer the following questions?

- Do you like your teacher? Why?
- Do you sing better than you did a year ago? Now go ask trusted others to answer that question based on their "before and after" observations of your singing.
- What have you learned about your voice since your lessons with this teacher?
- Do you enjoy the time in the lesson? Or does it make you anxious, dreadful, nervous, or bored? Explain your answer.

You deserve honest answers to these questions. Remember that you are paying for these services, one way or another. Even with a free-ride scholarship, you are paying with your time. Do not hesitate to question a situation that is not good. Before deciding to leave, you might want to speak with the teacher about areas where you feel you are not progressing. Write up a list of issues troubling you, and take it to your teacher. Sometimes the teacher can step up and make things better. If you are having a sour studio experience, it's best to leave. The mentorship relationship of singer and teacher is too intense, personal, and costly to hold onto it after it is no longer working.

Cults

If you're lucky, someday you will find a teacher who is excellent. You may meet others who have studied with this person who also had great results, and a group excitement may form. Forming a bond over a terrific training experience is wonderful, but please don't put any teacher on a pedestal and call them untouchable, the best in the world, or the master of the one and only true way. Your teacher is a human being. They make mistakes and have to wipe their bottoms just like the rest of us.

Again and again, I have seen people of all ages latch onto a teacher and say things like "this is it" or "I have found everything I need here." They fawn over the master and place themselves in a bubble that is no good for anyone. Adulation gets stupid rather quickly. It is not disrespectful to ask questions, to be a little skeptical, or to look to multiple sources for knowledge and skill. A teacher who tells you to stay close to them and not look outside of their circle is having ego and boundary issues. Don't go there, unless codependence and psychodrama are things you really enjoy.

Every excellent teacher will eventually be considered a guru-saint by one or more students. Some students will feel that their guru is the one and only forever. It's important for teacher and student to understand that, however perfect things seem to be in the studio, there are other people in other places doing wonderful things in different ways. It would be helpful if teachers would acknowledge this more. People who have had more than one excellent teacher tend to understand this. Those who have only had one good teacher, or very little experience in general, tend to be drawn into a more cultish allegiance.

One might think that we should be past such problems, with all that is now known about human behavior, history, and the modern concern for "fact-based pedagogy". But the human need to believe in something or someone whole-heartedly sometimes gets in the way of progress, rational decisions, and deep reflection. Unquestioning allegiance turns off our critical thinking. It is never wrong to keep your mind open and explore other ways. You can always circle back to your "tried and true".

Teacher, Not Therapist

As a singer, I am most comfortable with a teacher who is kind and respectful but does not try to get into my personal business. The boundaries are not strict, and different things work with different people, but it is a very common error for students to become too enmeshed with their mentors. By "enmeshed", I mean a desire to stay with a teacher due to personal attachments, to the detriment of your learning. Make sure that you are paying them for lessons that actually help you to sing, rather than their companionship or personal counseling. Only you can tell if learning has stalled and it is time to move on, but when it's time, it's time.

In my conversations with other voice teachers, it has often emerged that they are more personally involved in their students' lives than I am with my students. The amount of personal talk in lessons seems to vary a lot. It is very easy for "How are you?" to turn into a talk therapy session, if the teacher allows it. Some teachers feel that this is OK, because we are important people in our students' lives and that, in working with voice, we are already involved in a personal way. They maintain that if there is a personal issue that could be affecting the singer, we should discuss it to see if we can help somehow. That makes sense, and I know great teachers who work this way.

I look at it differently. I look at the voice lesson as a special sanctuary, where people come not just to learn, but to connect with something wonderful and unique about their humanity. Getting to the vocalizing quickly and with eagerness (at least on my part!) not only gets more done in the lesson, but it can also lift the mood of the singer. It can take the singer out of his problems and into a better place. Rather than discuss the boyfriend problem or commiserate about the lack of jobs or what nasty weather we're having, let's go to music. Let's sing. Let's go somewhere better for this hour.

If it's a "bad day" for the singer in any way—vocally, attitudinally, situationally—I will adjust the exercises and the work on the repertoire so as to build a scaffold of success, to the best of my ability. Sometimes, I need to be less demanding or taxing and more nurturing. I like helping in that way.

My approach of being less of a father or a buddy to my students than some other teachers is based on decades of teaching and on how I was taught (with both good and bad examples!). It is my goal to be sensitive to the student and offer a satisfactory, healthy singing experience, which will usually leave them feeling better than when they arrived. If I can accomplish that, I've given them a service that is at least as beneficial as talk therapy, and appropriate within my domain as a voice teacher.

We must stay clear about boundaries and know our comfort level from the start. It is better to start too formal and loosen up a bit later than to plunge into something more cozy than educational. The teacher should not only be the authority on singing, but also should lead in establishing the level of personal involvement that will most benefit the student.

Authenticity and Uniqueness

A big problem of modern singing instruction is the concept of "voice production" which often encourages a specific timbral ideal—a "kind of sound"—resulting in inauthentic vocalizing which distances the artist's individuality from their own voice. This problem is rampant in all genres. The line between sound and style disappears as a certain "sound" becomes "the style". Sound and style are not the same thing!

Examples of stereotypical stylistic characteristics, some relating to sound, some to a typical mood or vibe:

Classical: loud, dark, serious

Contemporary Christian: earnest, unrelentingly joyful

Pop: simplistic, trendy, not deep

Rap: cool and/or tough

Musical Theatre: exceedingly emotional, verbose

Country: common and folksy, nasal

People love authentic singing—singers who sound real and unique. I go with the old-time voice teachers here in terms of terminology—learning to sing is not the study of "voice production" but rather "voice cultivation". It's similar to how you don't produce a tree or a puppy—you grow it or raise it. Each of us already has a voice. It is up to us to develop its inherent potential. Put another way, just as we accept that each person is born with a unique speaking voice, each singer can and should have a unique singing voice, which can be developed in a manner that allows it to *stay* unique. Hurray!

If you learn how to sing freely, that is, easily and spontaneously, you will uncover your own true voice, and it will be unique. It's an ongoing project, because the voice changes through the years. Your freest voice is the voice you must learn to love. It is the only honest way to your own unique sound. You can self-consciously build a vocal persona as some try to do, but you will have more potential expressively and technically if you constantly grow who you already are by keeping the channel clear. This includes exercise and healthy habits of all kinds.

Style influences vocal quality and vice versa. A singer has to reconcile what they like with what their voice likes in order to make authentic singing happen. A music school curriculum can bring together pieces of what is needed, but it is up to the singer to figure out what works for the long term. All other things being equal, a country singer who grows up in a family of country singers will "find her own sound" at a much earlier age than a classical singer who falls in love with opera at the age of 17 and goes off to college to get a Bachelor of Music degree in classical voice. Time is required.

Similarly with "crossover"—someone who came up as a classical singer and falls in love with jazz will need to spend a lot of time, as in years, listening, experimenting, and messing up in that genre before they can begin to find their authentic voice there. Many yucky "crossover" albums are evidence of not having lived with the intended style long enough.

Imitation, per se, is not a dirty word. There are so many aspects of singing that we learn about this way: timbre, ornamentation, vowels, vibrato, nasality, dynamic phrasing, timing, and on and on. Imitation is part of the path to freedom. You don't TELL someone how to do a baroque *trillo* or an R&B riff; you SHOW them. You have to start somewhere, and people have been imitating what they hear for thousands of years—perfectly natural.

After the imitation phase, the "live with it" phase can begin. Only then can the singer's unique interpretation begin to grow.

Talent Shmalent

"Knowledge plus 10,000 times is skill." — Dr. Shinichi Suzuki, founder of the Talent Education movement and the "Suzuki Method".

Where ability comes from, whether inborn or acquired, doesn't really matter. Ability can be built through practice and study. Learning to sing is a constant process of uncovering potential. The human voice is very malleable. Today's ugly duckling of a voice can change radically for the better when interfering tensions are released, the vocal tract is used differently, muscles are coordinated, and new concepts of what is possible change.

I have had people with little knowledge of musical training tell me that what I do as a voice teacher doesn't matter at all. They insist that voices are born and not made. "You either have it or you don't." That is rubbish. I have seen too many examples of voices improving dramatically, including my own.

Every high-achieving athlete or performer eventually got to a point where they had to work hard in order to continue to succeed, where "natural aptitude" or "God-given talent" no longer matters. Time, patience, and intelligent work are great levelers in the real world of achievement.

Corporate Singing

The term "music industry" represents a problem. Well, many problems, actually, but let's discuss the vocal markers of some styles and the related technical demands on the singer. In many genres, we have standard markers that say "this is an operatic sound" or "this is country" or "this is rap". Some of these make sense, and some don't. In our zeal to categorize, we can put arbitrary limits on a singer.

Adding unnatural nasality to make a "more country" sound, imitating auto-tune acoustically to sound like a pop recording, or forcing the larynx down low in the throat for "classical" singing are examples of common techniques that handicap singers. Recordings and performances tell us that there are ways we "should sound" to be categorized correctly.

In the world of voice training, there are branded methods that have signature traits and sounds. Most of them claim to be teaching for the "music industry", but really, some of the sounds and techniques that are being taught are in a vacuum isolated from what real working singers need to do. They run the risk of thwarting originality by using formulas to sound a certain way for a specific style.

The internet has provided opportunities to hear performances from the dawn of recorded sound onward. In the opera genre, the further back you go, the more individual the singers seem to sound. Can we know for sure that uniqueness was more normal? Could it be that only the best recordings have survived and that many sound-alikes were never recorded? Perhaps, but I still think there is a big problem with people having prejudices, shaped by popular taste, about how they "should" sound, at the expense of artistic freedom and uniqueness.

In my vocal neck of the woods, classical, there is a desire for a certain kind of resonance that occurs from a low-ish larynx. Now, a low-ish larynx is generally good for maximizing acoustic energy in an unamplified voice, but it's **how** the larynx descends that is the problem. There is a large percentage of classical singers getting their "classical sound" by stiffening the base of their tongue down against the larynx, pushing it lower, rather than letting it go there in an easy suspension. Some of the so-called "child opera stars" and talent show "discoveries" have a lot of vocal problems from forcing the larynx into an unnaturally low position. Unfortunately these are examples to the largest number of people of what a "classical singer" sounds like.

I have judged auditions where college and conservatory singers are trying to sound like opera singers rather than learning how to maximize their *own* sound while keeping vocal flexibility and vowel intelligibility. It makes them sound alike in a sad way. It hobbles their spontaneity, agility, and expression and makes them sound old before their time. No young singer should ever sound old. Mature, professional, resonant, big—wonderful! But old—never! The beginnings of wobble are rampant among young classical singers, because they are locking their throats chasing "a sound" rather than finding their freedom. This makes me mad and sad because it is completely unnecessary and counterproductive to any long-term career goals.

In all genres from opera to soul to rock to musical theatre, young singers need to remember that their idols sounded very individual (i.e., in their prime, they did not imitate anybody). Trying to imitate anyone exactly for more than a short period of time can cause vocal trouble. Although audiences *expect* people to sound like each other when they sing the same music, they are also ready to be won over by a *new* interpretation, delivered by an artist singing with their own honest voice.

As of the time of this writing, there are legions of young people trying to imitate the chokes, chirps, alien diphthongs, and vocal fries of certain pop divas, the alluring darkness of some opera singers in their 40s who are teetering on the brink of vocal ruin, and the earnest bright-hyper-boyishness of the favorite young men of musical theatre.

You must be willing to be you. It seems easy, doesn't it? But people are led astray somehow, and they get caught up with capturing a sound that is not theirs. And then so many end up sounding the same.

Schools

If you are not concerned with getting a degree, it does not matter whether the voice teacher you choose works at a school or not. As I love to reiterate, it's all about the teacher, so it doesn't matter whether they teach in a conservatory, a university, a church basement, or a living room in a small apartment.

If you want to get a degree, and you want to do it in music, I would be committing a sin of omission if I did not say this:

There is getting a degree, and there is learning how to sing. You can try to get those to go together, but don't assume that they always will.

I will briefly go over the basic formal educational options, but the purpose of this book is related more specifically to voice itself, so I encourage you to look at the work of Matt Edwards (https://auditioningforcollege.com) and others as starting points for learning more about the process of getting into a college or conservatory.

There are two main categories of music schools in higher education. First, are the independent music conservatories, where the training of musicians is the main focus of the institution. The degrees offered may be the same as at a college or university, but the focus of the whole institution is creating performers, and to a lesser degree, teachers of music. The second main category is a department or school of music within a college or university. Some of these music training divisions are as large as conservatories, and some are even called conservatories.

There is a tremendous amount of overlap between these two categories of music degree-granting organizations. Historically, conservatories had a higher proportion of music courses to general non-music studies, and, of course, the colleges and universities offer a wider variety of non-music courses to take.

More important than whether it's called a conservatory or a music department is the size of the school, the competitive level, and the presence of a voice teacher who will teach you how to become a good singer. That last bit seems obvious, doesn't it? However, I have seen far too many students get all excited about "performance opportunities" and "getting into a great school", only to have a nonproductive experience in the voice studio. Your studio voice teacher is the most important part of your training— far more important than the institution you are attending.

At both types of music schools, the degree options are similar. Usually the undergraduate degrees are: Bachelor of Music, Bachelor of Arts (often with fewer music requirements), Bachelor of Music Education, and less often Bachelor of Science (education). Concentrations inside these degrees can include performance, theory, education, music therapy, composition, technology, and arts administration, to name a few.

It's highly important to visit the school, meet some faculty members, interview some students, and take a lesson with a couple of the voice teachers. You have to see if you like the teacher, whether their students are improving, and whether it seems like they have things to teach you. Ask questions in the lesson. Ask *everyone* questions!

After your undergraduate degree, you can be more concerned with solo performance opportunities and professional networking. At the undergrad level, you have to learn how to sing, first and foremost. Secondarily, keyboard skills are incredibly helpful for learning repertoire on your own and will save you a lot of money in coaching fees. If you are a classical singer, you also cannot overdo foreign languages.

An undergraduate music degree program is a rare opportunity to immerse yourself in music and develop basic skills that will serve you for a lifetime in the field. If you decide to go that route, commit to it fully while you can.

Not Schools

Before the last three decades of the 20th century, training was usually handled very differently from now. Many of the opera stars who dominated the scene did not have college degrees. There were very few "young artist programs" and graduate degrees in voice performance. There was a process of nurturing the young person's voice first and foremost, to prepare them for their first performing experiences, with careful guidance over several years before their eventual professional debuts.

Many singers would see their teachers multiple times a week, sometimes daily, for shorter lessons. This allowed for more supervised practice in the beginning years, which helped to instill and reinforce good habits more securely.

Now, it is standard to have one lesson a week. In a few music schools today, singers have two short lessons per week rather than one longer one. This changes the ratio of days of guided versus unguided practice from 1:6 to 2:5. In such a program, if a lesson is missed there will be another in just a few days. Having twice as many contact days per week allows for easier course corrections and shorter lessons allow for vigorous vocal exercise without tiring. If you are studying voice privately, consider asking your teacher if you can come for two half hours a week instead of one hour.

There is anecdotal evidence that young singers in the past worked on exercises much more than repertoire in their lessons. It seems that it was not uncommon for aspiring singers to work only on exercises, vocalises, and simple songs for *years* before attempting major repertoire. Today, if a singer is just beginning private voice study in college, they will not get this level of training.

The "teaching to the test" phenomenon is very prevalent, with the requirements for singing repertoire (in foreign languages for classical singers) for a faculty jury at the end of every semester.

In his book *Singing: Personal and Performance Values in Training*, Peter T. Harrison has proposed his ideal school for singers. His comprehensive course of study, including the more frequent teacher-student contact described above, is radically different from that which any modern music school offers. He includes structured exploration of literature, body movement, drumming, and non-singing performance including clowning, among other innovative ideas. He says that if we are going to put people through formal training programs to become performers, let's do it right, and give up trying to cram an artist's training into the framework of a traditional 120 credit-hour bachelor's degree.

Roll Your Own?

It is possible to not get a music degree and still become a well-trained singer. In the past, many great singers in many genres did not obtain music degrees. Only a few generations ago, opera singers with degrees were in the minority, and until a few decades ago, there was no such thing as a musical theatre degree.

The first and most important issue is to find a great voice teacher. Especially when you are young and green, you must prioritize learning how to maximize your voice from the best teacher you can find before worrying about perfect performing opportunities. Great singers will get a chance to sing when they are ready. Patience and long, steady work are not glamorous, but building success in any field is not glamorous.

You will benefit from learning to read music. It's no harder than learning how to read words, and it will help you immensely when you get work in the field. Along with reading, you should get a basic grounding in music theory. At least understand scales, chords, basic musical forms, and how to put musical ideas on paper.

If you are in the classical realm, you must study languages out the wazoo. You can't overdo this. A classical singer must learn how to not sound stupid singing Italian, German, Latin, French, and English. Everyone will have stronger and weaker languages, but getting a good coach will help you to fill in the gaps as you learn repertoire. You really should develop conversational fluency in at least one of the foreign languages in which you sing, preferably more.

A coach, or more specifically, a repertoire coach, is indispensable for some styles such as opera, art song, and musical theatre, and is very helpful for other styles as well. The repertoire coach doesn't teach vocal technique but instead, helps you with style, notes, text, musical effect, performance practice, rehearsing, and related topics. Sometimes, you will want to work with different coaches with different areas of expertise in fairly quick succession while continuing to study with a good voice (technique) teacher.

A Degree in Something

So, if you feel strongly that you want a post-secondary education, and you love to sing, shouldn't you just follow your bliss and major in vocal performance? Not necessarily. Many great singers did not get music degrees, and many music majors do not have music careers.

There is a 99% chance that you will not be able to support yourself with only singing engagements when you graduate from college, and something like a 98% chance that you will *never* do so. So, the way I see it, there are four basic approaches to going to college if you are a singer who wants a degree:

1. Major in something that will help you support yourself, and optionally do performance as a double major, a minor, or on the side. Majoring in something nonmusical which doesn't require too much physical labor or hours of talking every day can complement a singing career quite well. It can pay for your coaching, auditions, and other expenses with some left over for sustaining life. Michelle Markwart-Deveaux calls supporting your musical life with other employment "being your own patron". Brilliant!

2. Music education leading to a teaching certificate is by far the most popular of the singing-related majors. Keep in mind that teaching music in elementary and secondary schools requires much time, energy, and vocal effort, and doesn't usually pay as well as jobs outside of music. The first few years are exhausting, and you won't make it if you don't truly like it. Try to get some field experience as early as possible in your college career so that you can see what school environments are like. The classroom is very different from voice lessons. Some teachers love one and

51

not the other, so make sure you learn the differences first-hand and know your strengths.

3. Consider some of the other non-performance music-related degree programs. Music therapy, music technology/recording, voice pedagogy (focusing on private rather than classroom instruction), music business, and arts administration are some of the options available that may fit well with your performing.

4. Go full speed ahead in a vocal performance program, and concentrate on that to the best of your ability. This might be the only four-year stretch in your life when you can focus full-time on learning the art and craft of your passion for singing. If you are a classical singer, take as much foreign language as possible. No matter what genre you sing, learn how to play a keyboard. Study well, practice well, and absorb everything you can about the art and the industry. After graduation, you will either be that fraction of 1% who sing full-time or the vast majority who ask "now what?" and must consider a way to make a living. If you can deal with that reality, then go ahead and major in performance.

Strange fact: A music degree can work out fine even if you end up working in a field outside of the arts! Because technology and the pace of change in the workforce evolves so fast, even a computer science degree can be largely obsolete by the time you graduate. A particular major is not as important to many employers as whether you have a degree in *something*. In many tech fields, a music background is considered a plus. If a music degree feeds your soul and gets you through college and you end up working as a data analyst, that is *not* a problem!

Now, having said "maybe you should, maybe you shouldn't, life has lots of twists and turns" et cetera, what about those who

DO launch a full-time performing career? "Making it" is no guarantee of happiness. Long periods away from home, loneliness, unsteady income, low pay, frequent auditioning, and constantly learning new material are common challenges that can get old fast. Sometimes, being a full-time performer doesn't feel like success. Don't assume that anyone is automatically happier than anyone else!

The world requires us to be flexible. Most people, artists especially, will have several careers during their working years, sometimes multiple ones simultaneously. This is reality. Talk this over with lots of people, and realize that there are many ways to live a life with music in it. Find people who make music regularly (part-time, full-time, pro or not), and ask them about their younger years. You will hear a lot of great stories, all different, with very few straight roads to where they are now.

When I first published an article on this topic, I got some pushback. Some people thought it was "negative". Bosh! Reality just is. There are many ways to have a musical life, and getting a music degree is just one possibility among many. Almost any choice can be valid, as long as it is an informed one. So go inform yourself.

Video Instruction

Videos about how to sing can seem like a helpful idea. There are many, many voice teachers attempting to teach this way, but without real-time give and take, it is very easy to for the viewer to misunderstand what the recording is supposed to teach. There are some videos offering intelligent tips and ideas to think about. Many will bring up issues that you can take to your team for discussion, if you think they have merit for your own development. A really useful way to make something productive out of a video is to watch it with your teacher in a lesson and discuss what the video is trying to accomplish, whether it is something you need to be doing, and how your teacher would help you to do it.

Another good use of the video channels is to seek out performances by great singers. Study those people! What were their bodies doing—general posture, facial posture, limbs? What sort of vowels were they pronouncing? How did they shape a phrase? How would you describe their timing? How would you describe the sounds they were making? What makes a great singer great? How important is appearance? How did they make a song come alive and speak to their audiences? Make playlists of singers who interest you. Come back to the excellent ones repeatedly. Talk about them with your friends, teachers, and coaches and compare favorites.

Distance Learning

I use videoconferencing for teaching occasionally. There have been three situations in which I have used it:

- A student who I had originally taught in person was not able to be present due to touring, illness, or having moved away.
- Someone who wanted a short course of lessons to learn how to hire a local teacher in a more informed manner.
- Teaching other teachers who wanted to learn specific exercises and teaching techniques.

Some teachers and singers say all distance lessons are horrible, yet others do virtually all of their teaching online. I find it more difficult to teach online because I'm not getting as many small auditory and visual cues as I would like, and because it is impossible to accompany the student at the piano.

It seems to be the case for most singers that online lessons are more beneficial after you have significant experience as a voice student, rather than being a beginner. I have only had one online lesson as a student, and it was somewhat useful.

Continuing improvements in technology should help the videochat experience, but it can never be the same experience as two people interacting in the same location and acoustical space.

Trademarked Methods Aplenty

Some of the better known proprietary vocal methods include:

- Estill Voice Training™
- Speech Level Singing™
- Somatic Voicework™
- Complete Vocal Technique
- Institute for Vocal Advancement

These all offer certifications in their method. Most originally had a charismatic founder, who is revered and quoted frequently. I have had experience with three of the above methods. Each had some good concepts to teach, but I wouldn't pick any one of them as a sole source for voice training. There are also a heap of other trademarked methods, many being splinters and knock-offs of the methods above.

Voice training should mostly be one-on-one, with a teacher who can listen extremely well and prescribe customized exercises for the student's present singing. Some of the methods above allow for customization, and some do not. Most of the founding teachers of the above-listed methods had amazing ears and analytical abilities, which are conveyed to their followers unevenly at best.

When choosing a teacher, it might be nice to know if they studied or were certified in a certain method, but don't make a decision solely on that, because it doesn't reveal much about the teacher except that they had a curiosity about the method at some point. If a teacher is adamant about their method as the one and only answer to how to teach singing, be alarmed. A really good teacher, even one who is a disciple of a certain method, should have an open enough mind to realize that no particular method contains all truth until the end of time.

Of course, if you find a teacher who has no "method" but who does have a good track record of training successful students, go for it! It's all about the teacher, not the "method".

How Long?

"How long will it take me to sound better?" I get this question fairly often from new students. I tell them that after two or three lessons, they should know whether my way of teaching has something to offer them. They should be able to notice improvements in the first few weeks, not months or years. Significant and lasting improvement takes time, and we can keep looking to sports for analogous time, effort, and likely results. Somehow, many people (at least in the USA) tend to accept that sports take time, effort, and training, while not quite believing the same about superior singing and performing skills.

In order to select criteria to use to judge whether you are improving, it is important to be clear about your goals.

Can you do more, and more easily, than before? That one question sums it up, as far as training goes. Are you more comfortable in the extremes of your pitch range, do you have more options about dynamics, can you make clear vowels and form words in a way that works with your singing rather than against it? Does your voice move better? Are you singing in tune? How does it feel to you? Is it easier? Is it pleasurable? Do you feel more confident? Do you like your singing more than you did before? Are you making a type and size of sound that is usable in the genre of music that you sing? Have you made gains in how to prepare a new song or get ready for an audition?

After two or three months with a new teacher, some of these questions should be answered "yes". To learn more about a system for assessing yourself, see the description of the *Self-Assessment Protocol for Singers* in Part 4.

Before we get to self-assessment, however, let's explore "The Confusions" that follow. As you go through your training, you are going to run into challenges that are unlike those of instrumentalists, actors, or athletes, although singers have much in common with all of those. Identifying the most common puzzlers in vocal training will help you to know that you are not alone or crazy!

3. The Confusions

Paradoxes

"Simple singing is so beautiful, yet learning to sing seems very complex."

"The easier the singing is for the singer, the more impressive it is for the listener."

"As the voice becomes more able and free, it feels less and less like you are doing anything."

"Singing a beautiful soft high note takes as much effort as singing a loud one."

"Many who sing well have no idea how they came to sing well, making them rather ineffective teachers."

Learning to sing is full of paradoxes. Some are easy to spot right away. Others emerge over time.

My student "Hal" is a singer-songwriter. When he started studying with me, his voice was raspy and unfocused, with a hole in the middle where the upper and lower registers did not meet. He had a diagnosis of nodules but had received the blessing of his ENT (ear-nose-throat) doctor to take voice lessons. As Hal's voice improved, the advice and exercises I gave early on were not the same I gave two years later. As his vocal folds and singing improved, with the registers stronger and more coordinated, I gave instructions for further strength-building that might seem contradictory to those in the beginning of our work together.

Well, they ARE contradictory. For example, working on resonance issues with a constricted, raspy, recovering voice is not appropriate. Working on them with a healed, better-functioning voice usually IS appropriate, if the singer wants and needs that. Some of the exercises that I use to build more strength, or as a counterbalance for certain kinds of specialized singing, could actually harm a weak or injured voice, like Hal's was years ago. Now, they are what he needs for vocal health and balance as he builds endurance and a bigger palette of sounds for his musical expression.

Another way in which the concept of paradox figures in voice study is the personal perceptions of sensations felt during the act of singing such as "think down to go up", "the loud is built upon the soft", and "retain the sensation of inhaling while you sing".

Whether paradoxical instructions and concepts "work" depends on the individual. Trying to make a paradox happen can make you crazy. Some singers have a learning style that thrives with strange images and paradoxes, while others need "just the facts".

Eclecticism or a Hot Mess?

All knowledge cannot be contained inside one person's mind, one method's pedagogy, or one era's zeitgeist. Most singers will naturally acquire technical ideas from many sources. However, while exploring many methods, beware of consciously or unconsciously tending to "find" ideas that fit into what you already think you know. This type of data collection is confirmation bias.

In order not to fall into a habit of confirmation bias, you should study a method or approach that interests you in some depth. Try it for a while, attempt to understand its reasons for being, and take a course in it if it seems interesting. After diving in deep for a while, you are in a much better position to determine what you can use. If you learn some new things, that is a good sign. If you come out of the course saying "It confirmed what I already do", then you probably have not dived deep enough.

The new things that you learn in a specific program of study may not necessarily be for you, but if you understand them within the context of the overall method in question, you can move on. Don't reject an idea simply because it's different. Try it first, then decide.

When you find things that work for you, keep them. If you do this in a method-agnostic manner and find yourself using technical points from several methods or teachers with different approaches, then you can truly call yourself an "eclectic" student or teacher. However, if you hop from method to method, and claim that it all works and that it's all good, you are missing the ability to separate the nutty from the plausible from the useful from the brilliant.

There is nothing inherently wrong with being a purist either. If you favor one method after comparing it to others, you certainly have the right to that approach as your main way. However, there are many people who go through teacher certification programs or study with a teacher of a certain method who stop being open to anything else. That often leads to stagnation.

Although it's tiring to keep your mind open, it's worth it.

Breathing

"Breath is everything."

"Breathe from the diaphragm."

"He who knows how to breathe and pronounce well will know how to sing well."

Watching videos of successful singers of many styles will show you that some move a lot and others do not, with expansion and contraction in varying parts of the body.

Some teachers claim to hold ancient traditions of correct breathing. Some of the people claiming teaching lineages back to great teachers of the eighteenth century cannot satisfactorily explain why breathing was barely mentioned by any of the old masters. "Breath support" and, more recently, "breath management" are terms that developed mostly in the last century.

Singers' bodies vary according to shape, size, and coordination, and their apparent ways of breathing will also vary. Each singer needs to explore what works best for them. The same singer may move air differently at different times depending on what they are expressing, as well as changing body weight and health conditions.

The basic needs that all the breathing systems are trying to address are: getting air into the body easily, using the air efficiently for phonation, having enough air for the phrase, and, what I feel is the most difficult, not stiffening the throat and locking the larynx at any point in the breathing cycle.

I struggled for years with "breathing for singing". I would expand certain parts of my body and feel energized and big and good, but my singing was still veiled and held back. I believed that how one breathed didn't matter, because it didn't affect my singing much. What took so long to discover was that I'd never felt a truly released larynx, so I didn't know I was actually reinforcing tensions when I inhaled. Until I could find a way to breathe and expand my body and feed my singing with free air and a free larynx, I could not possibly understand what all the fuss about breathing meant.

Although free breathing is crucial, all the fancy breathing techniques in the world (and there are many!) will not address every vocal problem. Among the many things that might not be remediated with "breath is everything" work:

- poor vocal fold adduction
- the ability of the folds to change from tense to relaxed and thin to thick
- postural faults
- faulty start of the tone
- vowels that are warped
- pitch change
- resonance adjustments
- interfering tensions that may need special attention, e.g., lips, forehead, hands, throat constriction, tongue stiffness
- psychological inhibitions
- faulty concepts about the elements of singing

Here is where I think "breath is everything" comes from: When you are singing at a very high level, and good habits have been ingrained, there is little to concern oneself with other than taking a breath and saying something. The impulse to speak/sing automatically triggers the breath, and a phrase is inseparable from the breath that feeds it. To such a singer, breath may seem like the only consideration, and the rest just happens. If you are that singer, congratulations! If you are not, don't beat yourself up for not quickly breathing or supporting yourself to excellent singing.

Don't expect a year or four of "breathing lessons" to solve all of the vocal problems. By all means, do learn how to free up your body and get the air in and out easily. Develop awareness of a soft or tense throat. We have to keep solving each problem that comes up, breathing-related or not, but often the problem that is wasting our air is not to be found in the act of breathing itself. Often, as the folds get stronger and more flexible, or some other breakthrough happens, throat stiffness is released and breathing issues evaporate.

The people who solved their breathing problems with better phonation and the people who solved their phonation problems with better breathing may always argue about what should come first. It's not either-or! You will need to work this out for yourself, ideally with the help of a good teacher to guide you through options. Through practice and study, it is your job to get to the point where singing feels natural, like taking a breath and speaking. Then "he who breathes well, sings well" may finally seem true.

Support!

"Support" is easily the most abused term in all of voice instruction. Most singers just settle for the definition their last teacher used, whether they can explain it to anyone else or not. Most cannot. It's rather subtle to experience and explain, at best.

Support can refer to activity in almost any part of the body below the larynx during the act of singing. This can range from the base of the neck all the way down to the feet. It usually includes explaining how the breath is used. It goes by many names:

- breath support
- breath management
- breath control
- *appoggio*
- singing from the diaphragm
- diaphragmatic support
- abdominal support
- thoracic support
- proper air flow

My current definition of support is: the reliable means by which the air pressure is regulated for optimal singing. It includes both the way the thorax moves and the way the phonation is initiated and sustained. It is a holistic system that may be described by widely varying mental concepts that cause the most helpful reflex actions to take place.

Many believe that training control of the breath as a separate technique is valid, but you can never completely separate phonation and the air supply. What we have here is the classic "chicken and egg" riddle: balancing optimal vocal fold adduction and appropriate air supply.

If the vocal folds don't adduct all the way, the singer uses too much air and may think that he has a "breath control" issue. He may work on how to take in lots of air, and try to control the exhalation with ribs and abdomen, often ignoring the real culprit: lax, leaky folds. There are lots of safe, "ugly duckling" exercises for getting the folds to come together that work directly on that issue, but they scare some teachers and singers, who feel that perceptible "air flow" is always a good thing. One of my teachers started every lesson with "yawn-sigh" exercises which were useless for helping my under-energized larynx. Work on efficient, unmuscled adduction can proceed along *with* attention to posture and breathing, but treating "the breath" as a kind of religion unto itself can lead us astray.

Alternatively, we can have folds that come together too tightly, often with a tense and elevated larynx, creating bright, shallow sounds with limited expressive range. While "deeper support" or more "flow" is often prescribed and might help the sound and the mechanics *someday*, we must first work on getting interfering tensions out of the way. Sometimes the interferences are several layers deep. Once unnecessary "muscling up" is released, we can find a better suspension of the larynx and the Goldilocks "just right" adduction of the folds which will encourage the "just right" amount of exhalation.

If you are going to verb something, that something needs to be ready to be verbed. If you are going to "support", *what* are you supporting? Is your larynx vibrating well and efficiently? Do you have clear vowels and the ability to make vocal noise for a half hour without getting tired easily? "Support" apart from the thing we wish to support (a strong, flexible larynx that vibrates well) is meaningless.

Support is a personal thing that will feel different as your voice changes with training and age. While big singing will feel like the body is quite involved, it should never feel like bearing down to expel the contents of your lower GI tract, or like lifting a heavy weight (Some teachers actually use those concepts!). The folds are tiny and can make huge sounds with the quantity of breath it takes to fog up a pair of glasses. Support when singing well is much more about keeping the body open and poised than about pushing the sound out.

In *Your Body, Your Voice: The Key to Natural Singing and Speaking (2011),* author Theodore Dimon says this about the degree of pressure required:

"The notion, then, that in singing we create a supported column of air that involves greater pressure than during normal breathing is a fiction. When we breathe out normally, the rush of air is so great that the vocal folds cannot vibrate in an efficient manner or sustain a sung tone. The same is true when we hold the vocal folds closed and force the breath against them, which creates a pressed or strained tone. In order to sing, there needs to be a certain degree of pressure from the exhaled air—otherwise there would be no air flow and the vocal folds would not vibrate at all. But this flow needs to be less than during normal exhalation, which is why we need to decrease breath flow by controlling the exhalation and maintaining the openness of the ribs and diaphragm." (Dimon, 2011, p. 46)

That's a splendid explanation of why you cannot sigh your way to a bold sound.

When you are making a more vibrant, efficient sung sound, you are likely to find that your abdominal wall is a bit firmer than in regular, relaxed silent breathing. You may also notice that your ribs move a certain way, or that you have feelings in deep, dark recesses of your body. Many people run away with these facts and concoct elaborate ways of setting up abdominal and chest conditions that make things ridiculously complicated. Once singers are told to "engage" their abdomen in some way, they often push (blow too hard).

Dimon is very articulate and sensible about the worship of abdominal control of support:

"Because abdominal activity is the most obvious aspect of muscular action that comes into play to produce sound, singers tend to latch onto this region as the focal point of vocal support, when really the action of the abdominal muscles is only part of a much more global muscular activity." (Dimon, 2011, p. 53)

For a deep dive into the origins of the word "support", which came from the Italian term "appoggio" in the late nineteenth century, see "Lamperti and the Evolution of Appoggio (Support!)" in the Appendix.

The Sad Lesson

Kyle, a new student, entered my studio for the first time. This polite young man had just earned a degree in voice performance and music education at a major American conservatory. I said, "Let's start with a five-tone scale on 'Ah'." I played do-re-mi-fa-so-fa-mi-re-do on the piano and gave him an encouraging look.

He shifted his feet, his forehead wrinkled, and he sucked in a huge breath. His lips formed a sort of funnel. Finally, a muffled, dark, amorphous sound emerged like a bubble rising through a thick liquid. If a lava lamp could sing, this might be the sound it would make. This laborious pattern was repeated for each exercise, with an occasional restart and an "I'm sorry". With all that wind-up for every vocalization, I suspected that he was accustomed to receiving a long list of instructions about "tone production". Perhaps he was constantly reviewing that list as he self-consciously sang for a new teacher? Many questions popped up in my mind.

Kyle was obviously very bright and eager to learn but so tight and controlled from head to toe that loosening him up and finding easier vocalism was going to require a lot of time and work. The over-controlled, contracted, thwarted condition of his singing was hiding the potential for uniqueness, freedom, and high ability. I have seen this in many graduates of vocal performance programs. Some make it through with lovely, energetic, unique voices, but many more sound somewhat labored, lacking individuality, having learned how to manufacture "appropriate" sounds.

I love the work of helping any singer find their voice, no matter how compromised. However, many singers who have already invested a lot of time and resources in training in their current way find it difficult to change. They will hesitate, refuse, or mistrust the process of "undoing".

Did Kyle understand on some level that the complicated, over-cultured manner in which he sang was tying him up in knots? If so, was that feeling overwhelming? He did not return for a second lesson. Was that because he doubted my ability to help? Or was it just too onerous to deal with the possibility of change? I'll probably never know. Needing to untangle overproduced, labored, dampened vocalism after a bachelor's degree in voice makes me wonder what went on in the conservatory studio.

Squabbling Teachers

The internet has provided the opportunity for teachers from across the world to communicate with each other about teaching singing. The resulting conversations tend to follow some predictable patterns.

What often happens:

"We're both saying the same thing."

"Yes, that agrees with my experience."

"It's just semantics."

"Do you know who I am?"

"My teacher taught me all I know, and I really don't need to look any further."

"I'm going to show you what a nut job I am by irrationally fighting everything you say."

"You are a jerk."

"That is so wrong. It flies in the face of everything I believe."

What rarely happens:

"By golly, you're right and I'm wrong! I'm going to change."

"I think I see where you're coming from. Let me see if I have this right (restates what they heard). I'm going to think about that for a while and get back to you."

"I would love to discuss this further one-on-one and get to know more about your point of view."

"I don't understand. Can you please explain?"

"I'm not offended at all. I'd be happy to explain further."

"That's an interesting and different way to think about it."

Voice teachers work one-on-one, as did their mentors, isolated from their peers a great deal of the time. The attitude of "this sacred knowledge from my master is being passed on to you" passes through the generations, largely unquestioned. It creates rigidity, unchecked mutations, eccentricity, and just plain mistakes. Put two teachers together from different pedagogical lineages, and there are often sharp disagreements and drama due to an extreme lack of skill development in peer review and sharing. Voice teaching, being a "lone wolf" sort of career, can make a person a little weird to work with.

When observing teachers' disagreements, notice the *way* that they disagree as much as the content of their arguments. Would you want to spend years of one-on-one time with a person who expresses themselves this way? I am delighted when I can find someone to debate with who is cordial and respectful. Differences of opinion with such people is often a good learning experience.

If you change teachers at some point, and the new teacher says things that seem to contradict what you learned before, try to stay open. They may both be right, or they may both be wrong! Although it may not be comfortable, you will need to ask for clarification and perhaps explain that you are having difficulties with the new direction. Give them a chance to explain themselves. They might start to make sense or help you see multiple ways of looking at something or help you confirm that, in that particular case, you might stick with your previous instruction.

Great teachers do not, and will never, agree on all of the major aspects of learning to sing. There are many areas where most of them agree (mostly the "what" questions), but there is a huge variety in answering the "how" questions.

The Black Box

When we learn how to play the guitar or the piano or the clarinet, we have direct control of virtually all elements of sound-making and use of the body. We can feel and direct the actions of our hands, fingers, tongue, and lips. We can watch them in the mirror. We can feel and see muscles contracting and causing movements. We can see directly how the movements affect the music-making. These things are not true in singing. The vocal folds lie deep in our necks at the base of the larynx behind a wall of cartilage. The muscles inside and near the folds are not visible and mostly cannot be manipulated directly and easily.

Although it is challenging that we have so little direct sensory control over some parts of the vocal apparatus, human beings are blessed with the ability to make sounds automatically by mere intention. Developing new intentions that work with the way voices develop, as established centuries ago in the empirical methods of the old Italian singing masters, will lead to changes in the way the sound is made due to direct connections between the brain and the larynx. The path to freedom is not just based on making it sound "good"; it's based on making singing "easy". Many singers chase endlessly after their version of "good" and never get to freedom, ease, and cooperating with Nature—to make the most of what they have.

People sometimes try to reverse-engineer technique from sensations they feel in their bodies when they think they are sounding good. This is part of the puzzle. We can achieve finer control by also learning how to listen functionally, and learning what kind of sound-making will make a voice work better. With practice, you can hear which sounds move more easily, resonate more easily, begin and end well, and also feel good to make. When the voice becomes more agile and easy, we must go with that path and accept the resulting sound as our own, if health, ease, peace, and longevity are valuable to us.

Some singers cannot accept these ideas. They are attached to a particular kind of "opera sound" or "rock sound" or "dramatic sound" and will do anything to get those. Some try to control everything with various tensions that end up compromising freedom. Sometimes a student identifies completely with their story of how hard it is to sing. To such a singer, making things easier can feel terribly wrong, causing them to resist instruction and even quit lessons.

Easier singing can feel like better control with less control, more sound with less air, a big sound that feels small in one's head, a beautiful sound that sounds ugly to the singer, and so on. The perceived paradoxes are many, and some teachers rely on them heavily as teaching points, sometimes thoroughly confusing things. "Think down to go up", "The loud is built on the soft", "Engage the abs more to sustain a phrase, then even more to sing high, then even more to sing soft, then even more…" until the student is bound up in tension, stiffness, and confusion. The teacher is trying to convey what is right for him in his own body as he feels it, and the student is trying to understand from the point of view of someone who has not yet achieved what the teacher has achieved. That can be a big gap.

All of this confusion is because of the Black Box nature of singing. All the "voice science" in the world, all the imaginative ways of conveying sensations, all the mimicry you can muster, can't take you all the way to your own vocal freedom. You must find your own personal ways of working with Nature to elicit easier and more athletic vocal responses so that you can develop a healthy voice that responds to your musical and lyrical thoughts.

We can make the Black Box work for us by working with the natural direct wiring that we all have between brain and larynx— between concept and vocalization. A correct concept (input) leads to correct vocal function (output) in a way that seems magical, but it's not. It's cause and effect, worked out by singing masters long before the Industrial Age—not tactile or visible, but delightfully real nonetheless.

Is the Voice an Instrument?

Long ago, I thought of the human voice as an instrument, just in a different family than brasses and woodwinds and strings and electronics. However, I now think of flutes and violins and synthesizers as surrogate voices. There can be no doubt that music that used pitches originated with the voice, probably eons before the first external devices that we call instruments.

So what makes the voice "not an instrument"? First of all, vocal sound is made with the living tissue of a human being. There is no manufactured implement involved. Also, for the last few thousand years, vocal music has involved words. This element alone puts it in a completely different category from wordless music-making. Yes, there are a few pieces like Ravel's *Vocalise-étude en forme de habanera*, Rachmaninoff's *Vocalise*, and Gliere's *Concerto for Coloratura Soprano* that don't use words. In these cases the voice could be said to be like an instrument. But still the sound is made with a living human body directly and not with a manufactured object.

I think there are deeper reasons why the voice is not an instrument, in addition to the fact that you cannot separate the instrument from the person physically. The same voice with which you speak and cry out in pain or pleasure is the same voice with which you sing. It is primal. It is a deep and inseparable part of being human, not just a body. You cannot say that about a clarinet.

Sometimes singers try to get some psychological separation from their voices. They say "my voice" or sometimes even "the voice" when referring to their singing voice. A singer needs this distance occasionally to keep from being obsessed with its use and care all the time. There may come a time when a singer is unable or unwilling to sing, and having the singing voice be a thing apart from the speaking voice can make more mental and emotional space for the rest of life. In the case of the high-level performer, there is also a big difference between singing a lullaby for a grandchild and performing on a stage. These two scenarios may not use the same "voice" in psychological terms.

I get a strange, visceral, negative reaction to a singer talking about "my instrument" when they refer to their singing voice. It seems like enough of an objectification to say "my voice" or "my singing voice" or "the voice", but to say "my instrument" turns it into a machine to own and operate, and messes with my sense of the primal, true, human element that needs to be intact for one's vocal expression. Even in this strange era of alienation and technology, calling one's personal bodily means of making music an "instrument" feels wrong.

Correspondingly, I don't feel that "singing" is "playing an instrument" although both make musical performances. Singing involves a synthesis of expression that playing a tuba does not. The instrumentalist does not use elements of speech, hands, and face as part of the expression.

I have studied several instruments with the best teachers I could find. Every one of them encouraged their students to "sing" on their instruments. They all encouraged emulation of excellent singers. I have never had a voice teacher or coach ask me to play my voice more like a violin or saxophone, except for a novel, usually comedic, effect. And even then, I was still expressing words, which is a whole different world from playing a melody.

New Teacher, New Concepts

How can we quickly "crack the code" of a new teacher's vocabulary and teaching style?

If you have been fortunate enough to have a teacher who helped you acquire useful singing concepts, you are lucky! Alternatively, if by your experiences and brain power, you have figured out how to sing reasonably well even with confusing instruction, good on you! Either way, as you continue your studies you will probably work with multiple teachers and coaches and get all kinds of advice that may be expressed differently from what you have heard before.

Teachers who use terminology or concepts that are different from what you have experienced or what you can relate to are trying to do their best and may have much to offer you. However, you may experience frustration if you try to be a blank slate every time you work with someone new. It is up to you to get clear on what they are asking you to do. It is up to you to initiate a translation into terms that you can understand. It is up to you to decide what is useful. Ask questions!

When a teacher asks you to do something that seems strange to you and you have no idea how to do it, you need to do a little mental work to see if you can work with it, lest your big bucks for lesson fees go down the drain. Here are steps to follow when getting new and puzzling advice from a teacher or coach:

Ask yourself: Is the thing they are getting at similar to another thing that I worked on before?

If yes, try doing the thing you did before. If not, ask for more clarification about what they are hearing and what they are asking for. It may ring bells from your past experience. If it seems like a totally new concept for you, then you are in a position to be open to the possibility that this is new territory to explore. Go with the flow, take notes, and test the heck out of it at home.

If you have tried a new instruction to the best of your ability, and it went well, it's OK to tell the teacher, "We used to work on that when I studied with Teacher X. She used to call it '___' " if that is the case. This is useful information for your teacher, if they choose to accept it. It also will solidify your connection between what you have previously understood and what this teacher wishes to impart.

If you have tried the thing, and it crashed and burned, start asking questions! "Am I missing something?" "I don't think I quite understand what to do." "So what happened there?" "Maybe I'm getting confused with my interpretation of what you said." If you trust this person and want to give them a good trial, go home and see if you can work with their concept. If it makes no sense by the time of your next lesson, ask for clarification. The responses to your questions are how you will sometimes separate the wheat from the chaff in the field of teachers and coaches. An experienced, reasonable, effective teacher will welcome your questions and enjoy working for clarity in how you communicate in the studio. More autocratic, insecure, or ineffective teachers may be threatened by this and become defensive.

You may find that you can work with a teacher who uses a very different vocabulary and concepts from what you prefer/know, if you develop the ability to translate what they are telling you into the language that makes sense to you.

After a long time with one teacher, it can be very helpful to switch to a new teacher. With fresh ideas and perspectives, and simply by hearing new words, blockages can sometimes be broken down more quickly. This process of melding old with new, keeping the useful and discarding the non-useful, is a valuable skill you will use for the rest of your career—with conductors, band members, coaches, producers, and directors.

Such questioning, accommodating, clarifying, and even debating are also useful for peer-to-peer discussions of voice. Rather than throwing our guard up, why don't we count to 100 before responding to something we:

- don't understand
- don't like
- don't approve of
- failed at in the past
- have rejected for legitimate reasons

It's almost always a good idea to take time and respond slowly to strange new things, asking questions gently.

Melting Mysteries

Some teachers and singers relish the mystery. It keeps them coming back for more. If a teacher can give the student the impression that they are a wise and intuitive master with knowledge and ways beyond mortal understanding, they can create a hook that fascinates the student.

Singing is indeed a little mysterious. It seems miraculous how many sounds can come from one person. We can imitate other people, animals, the sound our car is making, and many other things, without being able to describe how we do it. There is a direct wiring between brain and vocal tract that causes reflexive action. We think a sound, and we make it without pausing to analyze the placement of tongue, lips, oral cavity, et cetera. The ancient singing masters understood this, as did such authors as Cornelius Reid, Oren Brown, Yvonne Rodd-Marling, Frederick Husler, Alfred Tomatis, and Peter Harrison.

As a rule of thumb, if I can safely demonstrate for a student, they will generally understand the point more quickly. If I can only talk about a concept but can't demonstrate it, it is less likely to be a clear teaching point. The demonstration does not have to perfect, but it must illustrate a point clearly. One of my coaches, a brilliant pianist but not a singer, would sometimes demonstrate a phrase vocally that was like a sudden rainbow of truth. Then I could run with it in my own singerly way.

Sharing impressions is not teaching how to do something, although it has its place in the process. The word "feel" is loaded and risky. "It should feel as if . . ." should be used very sparingly. For example, a teacher may say, "As you sustain that pitch, make a slight crescendo and feel your pelvic floor engage more. There, do you feel it?" If the students says yes, what does that mean? If they say no, what next? How can I ever know that I am feeling the right thing to the right degree for the right reason, the same as another person?

You have the right to ask questions in your quest to solve mysteries for yourself. If you teach, know that your students should do the same, and be kind. What seems self-evident to you may be completely baffling to someone else and vice-versa. Getting to the point of understanding each other is golden.

Something to Hang on to

A tiny baby will grab your finger if you put it in the palm of its hand. This is the "grasp reflex". The body has many such reflexes to stimuli. The grasp reflex, however, is a special one in terms of its metaphorical meaning. The English language is full of references to the need to grasp something. "Holding on by a thread", "needing something to hold on to", "can't let it go", "seize the opportunity" —all refer metaphorically to the primal idea of grasping.

When we are perplexed, we want an answer. We are more likely to accept a horrible answer than to have no answer at all. We hate the void. We want a thing to hold on to. We see this in religion, where some people need to have literal truths, while others can tolerate the concept of eternal mystery. People want to know what to believe.

Many singers, me included, have concepts that they hang on to as "the way": the way to sing high notes, the way to breathe, the way to articulate fast scales. However, when we decide that we want to improve one of those things we must do something different. We must let go of something that we have held. For some people, this is unthinkable unless there is something new to hold on to immediately. Others have a higher tolerance for letting go of the old before something new is available.

I encourage you to revisit the things you hold on to, and let them go for a time. It is a great learning experience.

For example, a voice with too much loose air in the phonation can often benefit from practicing glottal onsets for a while. But after the voice becomes efficient with the air, are glottal onsets needed all the time? Are other onsets now possible? Can the voice gain even further efficiencies by letting go a little and starting the sound "out of thin air", or in some other way that hasn't been tried for a while, or ever? It may well be that *now*, after remedial exercises, starting with a feeling of "breath first" doesn't make the sound breathy!

Another example: You may have been taught to take a breath "as low as possible" — fill your body with air right down to the babymaker. Then one day you have a phrase in a song in which you seem to run out of air, or there isn't time to breathe. What if you let go of the "low as possible" breath, and instead inhaled easily in some different way just for that instance? Would it hurt to try that? Can you go against what you believe for a while to allow newness?

There are "meta" ideas that voice teachers hang on to as well. One is "It would be great if we could all agree on a common terminology." I've heard this dozens of times. But is that true? How could we really know whether it's true? What are some ways that the opposite is just as true? How could a wide variation in terminology be helpful to learners?

I'm not saying "anything goes", and I loathe the sentiment "we all want the same thing", because we clearly don't and probably shouldn't. Instead, wouldn't it be groovy if we could freely discuss our different approaches and react to each with "Hm, that's different, tell me more about how you use that?"

Imagery and Mirages

For the present purposes, I'm defining "imagery" in singing as concepts involving images or sensations that are intended to help an aspect of singing. Usually, such concepts are used for a while in order to establish a new technical goal, then dropped when the desired technique becomes habitual, because thinking about a non-musical image while trying to perform would be distracting.

Why is imagery so popular as a teaching mode? How did we go from old pedagogical writings that never mentioned images and sensations to the modern day, where we have dozens of "methods" that contain varying quantities of imagistic concepts? It's my suspicion that there has always been plenty of imagery in the experience of singing, but it was known in ancient times as more of a by-product or checkpoint than the main method of instruction. The tools of instruction in the books of 200 years ago tend to stick to elements of music and text, with very few excursions into anatomy, kinesthesia, cognition, and sensation compared to what came later.

There are two ways that imagery may be a help. Both are indirect, but one is more direct than the other.

The more direct one is an image that triggers a **reflexive response** that leads to a better outcome. For example, thinking of creating the vowel under the vocal folds may help you to keep a more supple throat with a better suspension of the larynx. If it feels right and works consistently, keep it. You will possibly grow a large collection of images and sensations as you gain more experience working on your voice. These may be similar, different, or opposite to those that another singer has.

The second way imagery can be of use is **association after the fact**, which can possibly become a cue. This can also be called "stumbling on to a helpful image". This is where you do something good, and you notice a certain perception (usually a feeling or sight, but for some people also tastes and smells!) that accompanied the action. This perception is self-generated, spontaneous, and cannot be given to you by someone else. An example of explaining an associated image might be a statement like "When I hit a high note well, it feels like a beam of light shoots out of the top of my head". Bring such associations to the attention of your teacher. With luck, the teacher can help you to use the association proactively.

A teacher should never assume that a maxim about a certain imagery concept will be exactly what is needed. People are too different from each other to have the same result (vocally and mentally). It should be offered as one possibility, with the willingness to go another way if the suggested image doesn't work.

In the mid-nineteenth century, when we were first able to view vibrating vocal folds directly with the newly invented laryngoscope, we began to be obsessed with "seeing" the voice in action. During that century we also went from talking about "cultivating" a voice to "producing" it. We have to be wary of the temptation to turn the voice into a machine that must be managed. This is the case with many other modern "must-have" pieces of the mechanical system. Insisting that people "see" or "sense" things that were not observable before the rise of voice science is often unhelpful. Developing the cause-and-effect relationships among singing, hearing, feeling, and trying new concepts takes us toward greater growth and self-sufficiency. Technological crutches can get in the way.

Modern advances in the physical sciences, along with the ever-evolving fields of psychology, philosophy, and consciousness, seem to lure us further out on diverging paths. We create imagery out of the science, and we also cling to imagery that completely defies science, because we are eager for a way into the hidden inner workings of the voice. Exploring vocal function in an experimental, trusting, experiential way, taking into account the whole of the voice and the person, can seem so unspecific, but if we follow through over time, we can find the associations that work for each individual singer. Then the singer can feel in communication and ownership of their own voice, and "control" can be achieved by being in harmony with what is intrinsically right for **that singer.**

The process of finding one's own feedback (imagery, sensations, concepts) is unique for each singer, taking however long it takes. Telling all singers in a studio to go for a certain sensation, or to think of a certain image, is too general. While many singers may be able to proceed with a particular studio manifesto, others who have tried to do everything right without success can suffer needlessly. The teacher must be willing to tailor the message to the student.

Regardless of what I say, many insist that "Imagery works! Do whatever works!" But please consider that sometimes imagery works in ways that seem direct but may not be. Let's look at some possible ways in which imagery-based directives might cause change.

Scenario A

1. Teacher gives weird image-based concept, like "breathe through the soles of your feet" (example is from a real situation!).

2. Teacher sings the passage to demonstrate.

3. The student copies the demonstration.

4. Teacher thinks the imagery "worked", when really it's modeling better singing that actually worked, and the student found the same effect in her own voice. Sort of a positive bait-and-switch or "Do as I do, not as I say."

Scenario B

1. Teacher gives weird image-based concept, like "inhale the air all the way down to your genitals" (again, I did not make that up).

2. The student repeats the passage and sounds better because the student is: a) amused, b) grossed out, c) grasping at the meaning and trying to sound different any way they can. With any luck, those reactions take the student's mind off of an interfering thought or habit such as fixing the larynx low with the tongue, exaggerated lip shapes, pharyngeal manipulation, "technical checklisting", etc. In other words, the peculiar image disrupted a habitual behavior.

3. Teacher thinks the imagery "worked" when actually, it was the student being distracted away from a bad habit. Teacher keeps it in the magical toolkit and swears by it in pedagogy discussions.

Scenario C (a personal example)

1. A teacher demonstrated the following directive by having me feel his neck and then mine: "Sing your high notes through a wide lower neck. Widen the base of your neck on ascending intervals." (One that actually works for me as a singer, apologies to the functional purists).

2. I practice ascending fifths and octaves attempting to widen the bottom of the neck. I immediately like it and feel grounded and like I'm not reaching for the high note. The vibrato remains a constant shimmer throughout the phrase. The larynx just does what it needs to do. Is it because I was half-consciously manipulating it before and now I'm out of its way, or am I "doing something" right, or what?

3. As I continue to use the concept and think about why it helps, I suspect that this gets singers in touch with the "inspanning", or suspensory network of muscles, that Husler and Rodd-Marling describe in detail (Husler & Rodd-Marling, 1965, p. 24).

4. The teacher uses this concept with many students but has found that sometimes the image of a wide neck side to side helps, and with others, a deeper dimension front to back feeling helps. I'm still unsure whether I'm actually widening my neck, but I feel something different when I use the concept.

People understandably become attached to the concepts that serve them well, and then they tend to over-generalize. Because something has "worked" for a large number of singers, it becomes singer lore that you breathe through your hoo-hoo, shoot the high notes out of your crown, bear down poopingly for loud singing, and direct "air" to all sorts of strange places. However, many famous and successful singers don't believe in any of that. How can you explain that, except to come to the obvious conclusion that imagery is extremely personal?

There is another reason why the imagery-loving teacher may have success, if they are open-minded. By encouraging the faculty of imagination in their students, they are giving permission to think and experiment in ways that nurture artistry as well as technique. This gives agency to the student, which is beautiful! When the teacher is imaginative and flexible and encourages the student to have a similar attitude, working with imagery can lead to many discoveries, both whimsical and factual. An open-minded teacher tends to be a good teacher, regardless of their methods.

The imagery used in voice lessons can be a great help or a great source of confusion. It is a big topic that needs some airing. I encourage you to talk about it with your colleagues.

Mechanistic Directives: of the Devil?

For the present purposes "mechanistic directive" means: an instruction for a specific physical action in order to make some aspect of singing work differently.

Example: "Make a widening stretch in the soft palate when singing an ascending interval."

Such an instruction can be use useful if:

- it makes singing more beautiful with the same or less effort.
- after many conscious attempts which prove its worth, it starts to become automatic. The body usually likes to move toward greater freedom and collects happy habits rather quickly. Bad habits tend to take longer to accumulate.

It can become Satan's playground if:

- after hundreds of repetitions, you can't do it without commanding yourself to do it. No one should have a permanent to-do list to ponder every time they sing a phrase.
- it creates a new problem.
- it makes singing feel more difficult, regardless of the sound.

If our body-minds have never done a particular desirable thing, we obviously need to create a first experience before we can move toward that thing. Getting ourselves to feel and remember ANY new experience is a clunky process. Physical experience is not conveyed strictly by ideas and words, but they can be a start. Sometimes you have to jiggle something loose by any (harmless) means necessary. If a "do this" directive doesn't work after a few days' effort, throw it out. If you see something working for others but not for you, get more clarification and try again. If it is still a dead end, reject it for now. There are probably dozens of other ideas to get you to the same place.

One tricky thing about mechanistic instructions is that something that does not help now may work for you later. I have eaten so many words over the years that I will never go pedagogically hungry again. Of course, some advice is simply stupid forever.

Sensation and Sound

"Don't listen to yourself! You have to sing by feel, not sound."

"It is essential to listen to yourself."

"It will sound ugly in your head when it sounds good to the audience."

What can these mean? Do you listen to yourself or don't you? Why can't people agree on this?

One of the key problems with hearing oneself is that we hear both through the air and through the bones of our head. This two-stranded audio stream creates a very different sound from what the audience hears. It causes us to make sounds that are not quite what we intended and can lead to comments such as:

"He is just singing for himself rather than for an audience."

"She has no idea how incredible she is."

"Why can't he hear that (hideous timbre, bad vowel, change in resonance, etc.)?"

There are two main reasons why people say "Don't listen to yourself". The first is that the sound we hear is not the sound the audience hears. The second is that there are times when we sing in ensembles or with loud instruments and can't hear ourselves clearly, and must rely on other senses to help us to deliver vocally. I sang a choral job once with a woman who had sung in the Chicago Lyric Opera next to Birgit Nilsson, the famous Wagnerian soprano. Ms. Nilsson told her that there were times when things got loud on stage which required her to sing by feel because she couldn't hear herself. If someone with one of the most powerful voices of the twentieth century had to go by feel sometimes, then it's certainly something we all need to consider!

"It is essential to listen to yourself." is a logical directive. Singing is an auditory art, and wouldn't listening be a crucial part of our singing naturally? Some say yes, while others give a more nuanced view, saying that we must not take what we hear from ourselves at face value—that listening to ourselves has some complicating factors. Yes, we are going to hear ourselves anyway, so we might as well listen, but we must realize that self-listening is a separate skill from listening to other singers.

"It will sound ugly in your head when it sounds good to the audience." This reminds us again that the sound we hear at the time of singing can be very different from the sound that the audience hears and also different from what we hear on a recording. Self-confidence and self-esteem issues can warp our hearing, both in the moment and when listening to recordings of ourselves. On the other hand, there are good singers who say that the sound is raucous or small or screamy or ridiculous in their own heads, but they have made peace with it.

This is all part of the strangeness of carrying our "instruments" inside our bodies! Working with a teacher and/or someone whose ears you trust completely will help you to reconcile what you are hearing and feeling on the inside when you are doing your best singing.

Fighting Words

Does each pair of words below represent polar opposites that make sense to you?

bright/dark
simply speaking/free-flowing air
reed tone/flute tone
chest/falsetto
chiaroscuro
ee/oo
brilliant/somber

Either "yes" or "no" is correct depending on the context. Your personal context is everything. A teacher should use a vocabulary that makes sense to themselves first and then communicate that to the student as clearly as possible. However, do not believe that the teacher can always get the student to think exactly the same thought from the same words. Such is the nature of interpersonal communication. Agreeing on words is less important than agreeing on concepts.

Whether a student is grasping a concept will be apparent by how the student sings after applying a new concept. The teacher should circle back and make sure that the student can link the new behavior to the new concept. This assumes that the concept was a helpful one to begin with. Be ready for surprises! Often, I have given an instruction, after which the student has sung better, and then I ask "What did you do differently?" Then they tell me something quite different than my original instruction. People interpret. It's natural. Sometimes we use different words to get to the same thing. Sometimes we apply the same words and get different results.

Is it hopeless to try to convey concepts with words? Not at all. Words are powerful tools, but we must stay humble and realize that they take on a life of their own in the other's mind. Sometimes our words only work when combined with something the student brings to the lesson from their previous experience or their present creativity. A student is rarely a blank slate. Check back with students frequently, and have them describe what is going on in their minds when a change has taken place.

In spite of the interpersonal interpretive gap, standardizing one's teaching vocabulary makes sense as a communication strategy in the studio. Using words consistently opens doors and gets you closer to your destination. When words fail, remember that the concept can be stated many different ways, and do not try to force an understanding that hasn't arrived yet. Be flexible.

How singers and teachers talk to each other about singing outside of their own studios is even more tricky. Conversations that use what seems like harmless terminology can lead to arguments and misunderstandings between people from different backgrounds. People certified in Method A say that Method B is bad, while those devoted to Method C laugh at the other two groups. The devotees of Madame X scoff at *all* the methods; methods are for losers! In these arguments, some teachers shut down, while others fight for attention like spoiled babies. It gets old fast.

If you keep your mind open for a few years and expose yourself to multiple master teachers and coaches, you will not only learn many things generally but also start noticing patterns among many of them. "Gee, it sure seems that a lot of teachers talk about the vocal folds needing to come together without wasting air." "Guru A and Madame X both seem to talk about lengthening the spine like they do in Alexander Technique." "What Mr. Z calls 'voix mixte' sounds like Dr. Q's 'mezza voce'." "Are the terms 'mix', 'register coordination', and 'ratio of chest to falsetto function' mostly similar or quite different from each other? Which one is most correct?"

Consider rephrasing what you hear in terms that you have already learned. Dare to draw parallels. Feel free to redefine a concept as an amalgam of all you have learned. Ask for clarification from the source to help you sort it out. Translate to the language that speaks best to you. Take it to the dressing room and try it on. Some things will look good on you; others may just make you look dumpy.

If you reject well-meaning people who speak a different language, you will miss out on many learning opportunities as both a teacher and a singer. Be bigger. If you are relatively new to serious voice study, I encourage you to seek out at least one different point of view from what you currently know, and find the commonalities and differences for yourself. No one person is the perfect teacher, and there is no perfect method or perfect "school". If you look outside of your present experience, you may find something better, or you may realize that you already have something very good. Win-win.

Verbs and Bad Teaching

*"Support should **feel** like you are bearing down slightly on the pelvic floor."*

*"High notes **are** not really higher; they **are** just faster."*

*"Pianissimo **is** a color, not a volume."*

*"The second formant needs to **be** stronger for that pitch and vowel."*

*"When your larynx is free it will **seem** like you're doing nothing."*

Definition of a *linking verb*: "a word or expression (such as a form of *be, become, feel* or *seem*) that links a subject with its predicate." (*Linking verb*, merriam-webster.com)

Linking verbs are necessary to describe things, but they are not entirely reliable words to teach with. If a teacher depends on description and "feeling" and "being" phrases without actual exercises to get you there, run! It's fine to share with other singers what you feel and how things seem to be in your own body and mind, but in order to get someone to do something new, you have to teach *how*. If you go to a teacher who does not directly address the "how to" for problem-solving, what is the point of lessons?

I am sparing in my use of imagery, but a directive like "Inhale as if you are pleasantly surprised" is miles ahead of a description like "the palate should be high on the inhale" because it is combining an action *with* imagination to get at a reflexive response rather than just describing a condition or location. Even "sing the vowel down into your chest while feeling the vibrations in your sternum with your fingertips", though vague and indirect, may get at something helpful, however stumblingly.

The "how" can be a tad weird or esoteric, but a "how" must be given! Merely describing desired feelings and conditions puts a burden on the student to come up with how to fix them, which is unfair. After the description of the desired outcome must come action. That means one or more targeted exercises.

If you want to be the best singer you can be, you have to get to a teacher who can help you with *how* to improve. A great model is nice; an informed critic can describe your faults and strengths; voice science experts can show you marvelous facts. However, there is no substitute for a teacher who is versed in helping singers and can offer multiple exercises and approaches to solving vocal problems.

Ask a prospective teacher questions that will give you a feel for whether they *like* solving problems. Do not be dazzled by an introductory lesson full of "should" and "should be" and "feels as if". We need action items in order to train; therefore, clear instructions for how to attack specific problems should be part of every lesson.

You Can't Cover Everybody

Let's say that you are a young singer in a good band. You start working, playing nightclubs, BBQ joints, any place that will pay you. You cover lots of songs and lots of artists. You come in for a voice lesson and describe your challenges to me. "When I sing Eleanor Rigby, I have trouble getting to McCartney's high notes, and when I sing Bat Out of Hell I feel like I don't have enough grit in my voice and when I sing Sam Cooke songs I feel like I don't have the right old school feel." I have to say "Whoa there! How many styles and bands are you covering?" The answer is almost always "too many"!

We must remember this: Cyndi Lauper had to learn to do Cyndi and stick with that. She doesn't do Cher and Beyoncé and Pink. She works with her own real self. Elton John didn't make a career out of doing Elvis impersonations. If you do lots of covers, you eventually need to get past mimicry and make those songs your own, singing with your own best voice.

Many singer-songwriters will find singing their own material more comfortable because it was born through their own voice and never had to be translated from another singer. However, a cover can be a great project for growth as an artist. One shouldn't be afraid to take someone else's hit and re-work it, in *their own* authentic voice. The performance will not sound exactly like the original artist; this is not a problem! Whether you are singing punk or classical or ska, you do you!

Health versus Your Sound

Imitation may have gotten you started singing. With luck, listening to good, healthy sounds was a naturally positive part of your learning. If all went well, you kept improving over time, and your unique voice asserted itself as you matured.

Over time, we learn to identify with how we sound, and we expect to keep sounding the same indefinitely. You could say that we imprint ourselves with our unique voice. This imprinting can be hard to override when things change.

At some point, we may encounter unwelcome changes with the effects of illness, injury, misuse, or lack of use, making our voices "worse".

There comes a point in your vocal maturity—it could be age 17 or 70—when you must choose whether to prioritize vocal ability and health, or making a certain kind of sound. Most people are willing to adjust to the sound they make if it is easier, more flexible, and lets them keep singing longer. However, some people are in love with a certain sound and try to imitate or maintain a certain voiceprint regardless of ill effects to their health, longevity, and career.

If your voice is highly functional and free and healthy, and you accept whatever "sound" that comes with it, you will be in a better place psychologically than insisting on sounding like someone else or even how you yourself sounded 30 years ago. Young singers are sometimes tempted to sound older, and older singers want to sound younger! Beware of these blind alleys. Train the voice, keep it strong and healthy, and love what comes out. The sound that works is the sound for you. A well-used voice is inherently beautiful, always.

Voice Science, Academic Religion

University and conservatory music departments looking to expand their relevance and build academic muscle are besotted with technology as a "relevant" add-on to their course and research offerings. Many voice professors now talk with missionary zeal about the biological, mechanical, medical, and acoustical aspects of voice. There is hardly a better tactic for improving the tenuous position of the arts in academia than by building up their relationship to the "hard sciences".

I went to a presentation by a well-known voice teacher turned scientist. He placed electrodes on the necks of several singers and showed us measurements of laryngeal activity on a computer screen. Then he had a master class with those students with their current repertoire. The class was awful. Whereas he claimed to be better equipped to help the singers with improving vocal function, he relied on vague and unscientific advice about "support" and "resonance" and seemed not to hear things that some of us felt should have been addressed immediately. I didn't see clear diagnostics leading to logical, actionable remediation. It was as if the technology had deafened him.

We need to be clear about how to bring a scientific observation back into the whole. How is it useful? How will we put the knowledge into practice? How does the incorporation of this knowledge further our art?

There are so many issues with trying to bridge between the scientific and performing worlds that it is hard to know where to start. Here are a few examples:

- It is tricky to know what value to derive from observing and describing processes in isolation that never actually occur in isolation.
- Students of good teachers who are well-versed in voice science don't seem to be singing any better than good old-timey teachers who used their naked ears and eyes exclusively.
- Science and functional pedagogy seem like they should go together, but they are separate fields needing separate study. Knowing science does not make you a whiz at eliciting vocal function, although it might help you to document what happened after the fact. Functional pedagogy is empirical. Reid (1965), Husler & Rodd-Marling (1965), Garcia (1847), and Tosi (1743) all described functional pedagogy. Master patterns of pitch, vowel, and volume. Find healthy body alignment. Eliminate interfering tensions. Train your ear to hear very fine differences that relate to conditions of a voice. Have a concept of the sound in mind. Know by hearing, observation, and trial and error what causes what.
- Voice scientists can make accurate observations about the properties of singing, and many can also elicit specific desired properties in themselves or singers, and still the result can be dull. Why? If we believe that we have all of the ingredients of good singing, what is going wrong with the result? How can someone with perfect formants and proper "registrational events" fail to move us? I believe that what is missing is a spontaneous musical response. When the spontaneous response is abandoned for a mechanical control, the singing suffers, but only about 99% of the time.

Acoustics, physiology, and biomechanics are all nice to know, but due to the Black Box phenomenon, they do not help us train singers directly. It's virtually impossible to go directly from the measurable scientific findings to teaching actual singing without strong training in both. I believe that many modern voice scientists are barking up the wrong tree. The branch of science that most applies to applied singing and performance is psychology. Singing is a mental and conscious act. Concepts and intentions and emotions have huge implications for vocal expression. The voice responds reflexively to these concepts and intentions, thoughts and feelings. Tissues and cavities that are not visible (and only partially perceptible) cannot be completely controlled by voluntary muscular action. Cornelius Reid touched on this in his books, as did David Clippinger, David Taylor, Edward Foreman, and Alfred Tomatis.

There is a direct connection between the brain and the larynx that allows us to make all kinds of sounds by just willing them into being. How much of that is understood? Isn't that a tad more interesting and a whole lot more applicable to real singing than interpreting the visual representation of a sung tone on a computer screen?

The old masters of the empirical (trial and error) methods of voice teaching concentrated on the mental control of the voice and brought vocal ability to a high level with discriminating ears and scrupulous command of the musical elements of vowel, pitch, volume, rhythm, and intention. They understood how to work with Nature—especially human nature—to strengthen, coordinate, and "bring out" a voice.

The old-time voice teachers—before the laryngoscope of the 1840s, before the introduction of "breath support" and "imagery" of the late 1800s, long before the voice science labs of the mid 1900s— knew that you could reach the voice where it lived and train it there. The voice is born and lives at the intersection of mind and vocal tract, a functional whole. For hundreds of years, singers were trained to very high levels without a knowledge of laryngeal anatomy or scientific measures of any kind.

Voice science has become an industry and is the way that many professors will achieve recognition and help their employers' reputations. The current adoration of the "hard sciences" in vocal pedagogy will probably continue for a long time. Meanwhile, back in the studio with aspiring singers, many of the same teachers resort to the same concepts of breath management, support, and imagery that their teachers taught them. The study of aerodynamics, biomechanics, acoustics, neurology, and anatomy serve to "justify what they do in the studio". The science-inspired teachers translate between the weird concepts they were taught and the esoteric facts they learn in the lab, and yet the singers are not better than they were before music schools acquired laboratories.

Psychology, learning theory, explicit listening skills, teaching methods, historical pedagogy, acting, physical fitness, listening to great singers, and music criticism would all serve students so much better than building clay larynxes, being able to point to the infrahyoid muscles on an anatomy chart, and highlighting the second formant on a spectrogram. Voice science is nice to know, but you can't do science. We are neglecting opportunities to train singers in how to listen, learn, and experiment with what they hear as singers and musicians. Singing is an aural art, which means that extremely refined listening skills are essential. Let's take listening as far as we can and see what happens.

4. Where Am I?

How good a singer am I?

Am I improving? How can I tell?

Am I on the right track?

This section deals with figuring out how you're doing. The human voice, being so individual, is impossible to standardize (thankfully) but that doesn't mean that we can't become aware of our current abilities, progress, and potential—technically, professionally, and emotionally.

In the first three essays, I will go into some depth about how to test your singing abilities and chart your progress. There has not been much written for singers about how to do self-assessment and record progress. Here, I propose a detailed, step-by-step system for doing that.

The last two essays are about handling feedback from others.

The better you know yourself, the better you can deal with comments, advice, and general feedback from the world.

Self-Assessment Is Crucial

Being able to determine whether you are improving is crucial to becoming a good singer. A clear understanding of your progress will help you to determine if you are on the right track and what you need to work on. You can then take these observations to a teacher and address them.

Many of us have heard the advice, "Don't compare yourself to everyone else, and focus on your own growth." Yet we have few alternatives to competition rankings, audition scores, school juries, and casting results as the primary ways in which to receive evaluation. By using a repeatable self-evaluation tool over time, singers can begin to chart their own progress and work on their issues more logically and confidently.

The Self-Assessment Protocol for Singers (SAPS) has been developed for recording oneself periodically via audio and video media, with directions for documenting the results of each test. It consists of three main parts. The benefits of the SAPS include the following:

- Students can feel more sure of progress, or the lack of it, and begin to take a self-advocacy role in their vocal study.
- Students and teachers can better refine the purpose and progress of voice lessons with clear goals for skill development, leading to "study with" rather than "take from".
- More experienced singers can use the protocol as a starting point to make decisions about criteria for skill development for their own situations and career tracks.
- Clearer descriptions and measurements of successes and failures in vocal mastery become possible at all levels.

- Singers can develop a sense of comparing former and current versions of themselves rather than only comparing themselves to other singers. Both types of comparisons are useful for professional development.

Contents of the SAPS

The two documents comprising the Self-Assessment Protocol for Singers (SAPS) are available at sanesinging.com/saps. Below is an explanation of the protocol's six parts.

<u>Recording</u>

Six tasks are recorded, using the **SAPS Instructions** document to assess the current state of these technical areas:

- agility—ability to move through many notes quickly and accurately
- pitch range—how high, how low, and the relative strengths of high and low pitches
- pitch change—ability to get from one pitch to the next smoothly, accurately, and easily
- dynamic change—how loudly and softly one can sing on notes throughout the range, using the *messa di voce* exercise
- articulation—including staccato, legato, and portamento
- vowels—degree of intelligibility, clarity, and modification for high pitches

After the technical tasks, a complete piece of repertoire is recorded. This portion is more like a typical audition or concert situation. It may be recorded at a live performance if the video and sound are good.

The singer studies the resulting recordings and records comments and scores with the **SAPS Scoring and Comments** document. The scoring and commenting process deals with such measures as technical ability, language, expression, artistic effect, confidence, comfort, alignment, physical ease, and satisfaction. At the end is a section containing prompts for the singer to write free-form comments and notes for improvement.

Being a singer-centered, personal process, if you need to alter the SAPS due to vocal challenges, time constraints, or special needs of any kind, please do! For best results in the future, take notes about what you did each time so that you can compare your results over time accurately. Feel free to give feedback about how you have made SAPS work for you.

<u>Description of the Tasks</u>

Task 1 is based on the second *Gorgheggio* from Rossini's *Gorgheggi e Solfeggi*. It is a basic agility exercise. The first note of each triplet is a step in the major scale.

The rhythm of Task 1 can be altered to linger on each step of the scale if desired.

Task 2 is Rossini's twelfth *gorgheggio* as originally written. The entire exercise stays in one key, rather than modulating for each arpeggio. This sequence contains major, minor, and diminished arpeggios.

A simpler alternative ascends chromatically, with a pause for each modulation:

Task 3, here called "Dynamic Changes", is the famous *messa di voce* exercise from the old Italian tradition. It was usually the first exercise given in eighteenth and nineteenth century books on voice training—an important point to ponder. A wide range of tempos can work. Start with quarter/crotchet = 120 if you are new to this, then slow it down.

Task 4, "Pitch Connections and Range", is the longest and most complex in terms of what is being evaluated. The term "vocal range" is defined here as the set of pitches that one can sing more or less smoothly connected to the rest of the range. The exercise should be done with a slide (*portamento*) between each slurred note. Singing each bar at three dynamic levels will test the connections among different pitch areas of the voice. Limits will be exposed here, since the exercise is to be done throughout the singer's range.

Task 5 is called "Vowels", and it uses contrasting articulations, as well as the five "cardinal vowels" of Italian and Spanish. The exercise is sung at any comfortable volume with each of five vowels, both legato and staccato. On playback, the integrity of the vowel sound can be examined, while noting freedom or difficulty with different vowels. Patterns of vowel migration may emerge, for better or worse.

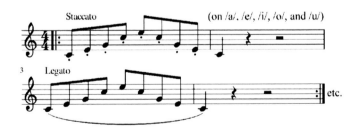

This task has a simplified alternative, which uses an arpeggio with a shorter range:

Task 6 is a video recording of any song or aria of the singer's choosing. It can be *a cappella* or accompanied. Ideally, the recording would use two cameras to show views from both the front and side, although an adequate compromise could be to place the camera at a 45 degree angle to the singer's face. Evaluating posture from different angles can be useful.

Daily Technical Check-In

It's a good idea to frequently check the basic functions of your voice to make sure you give it the exercise it needs to stay in shape. This is especially true if you are in a period of growth or exploration. For example, greater "cut" with less dynamic range and agility is not a good trade-off. Advancement in one of the main technical areas should not handicap the others.

How to check in? Use vocalises containing the following functions:

1. Quick pitch change (scales, arpeggios, and trills). If you can't do a trill yet, keep trying, as it can teach you things. Also try many scale and arpeggio patterns, perhaps rotating through different ones throughout the week.
2. Dynamic change (the *messa di voce*). You may have never had much dynamic wiggle room on your highest notes but you want to make sure that most of your range can be sung at varying volumes. I know it sounds crazy, but working on dynamic range tends to give you more dynamic range.
3. Ease of pitch range (high, middle, and low notes intact and connected to each other).
4. Staccato and legato note transitions. Staccato is very underutilized by many singers, but it's gold for checking the efficiency of the start of the sound—what used to be commonly called "attack" of the sound. I'm fine with the word "attack". It implies action and life. "Onset" reminds me of the start of a disease. With students, I usually just say "how it starts".
5. The five cardinal vowels of /a/, /e/, /i/, /o/, and /u/. Other vowels can also be used, but these are the basics.

You can use the SAPS as described earlier, or there are many other options for a consistent, structured check-in. One of my favorite thorough yet compact sets of exercises is the Rossini *Gorgheggi e Solfeggi*, available for free in the public domain. You can construct your own exercises that are similar to those, using the five principles above. An ascending and descending 9 note scale can be a good structure with which to work, if done in two or three different keys. See below for an example of such a C scale with four different rhythms.

If you are a singer of coloratura or riffs, practicing a difficult run with all of the rhythms above will help you to become very technically secure. Transpose the scale up or down as needed to work out the different pitch areas of your voice.

Generally, do most of the exercises with the /a/ ("ah") vowel and its near relatives, and occasionally check in with other vowels. Each vowel has something to teach your voice. Many people, in their quest to sound more impressive, will develop warped vowels, or merge them into one all-purpose non-vowel. A warped vowel wrecks your diction, lessening the impact of your lyrics, and it can also be harder to project, falling out of the mouth and dying a few feet from the stage. As pitch rises, the vowels can change, but they should always sound human. That may seem sarcastic, but listening to auditions all day can make you wonder about that.

Checking in daily with the five basic functions above, regardless of the specific form of the exercise, will help to keep you on track. All of these checks can be done in less than 15 minutes, if necessary.

If you ever find yourself in a situation where you have to warm up very quickly, experiment to find what works best for you. Some people need to move the voice, some just do a few quick sirens, lip trills, vocalizing through straws, or other exercises that do not use an open mouth. If I'm in a five-minutes-or-less situation, I will wake up my throat with a couple of sirens from high to low and low to high, and some form of the *messa di voce* (soft-loud-soft on one note).

Usually, I do the *messa di voce* over about an octave and a fifth. As a tenor, I often warm up on the pitches from C3 to G4. This helps me to get to the core of my voice quickly. It exercises the thin-to-thick-to-thin fold function, which relates to high-low function, which relates to flexibility, which relates to everything else. A *messa di voce* on just a few notes in the middle of the voice can be an effective, fast warm-up when necessary. If I have a little more time, I will do some light staccato arpeggios as well.

Time and experimentation is required to figure out what works best for you. There are two main things to consider when you check in:

- What kinds of warm-ups get my voice flexible and ready for anything?
- What kind of music am I going to be singing today?

The warm-ups you need to wake up your voice and get it moving are often very different from the music you are going to sing.

The Advice of Other Humans

Earlier in this book, I mentioned the singer's team. It is extremely helpful (mandatory if you have professional aspirations) to sing regularly for your teacher and coach and other trusted ears. You need to sing a lot for real people in order to grow.

A coach can help you to find specific repertoire that works best with your voice. Your voice teacher can monitor how your voice is doing with your performing demands and suggest the general types of repertoire to explore with a coach. A musical director or conductor can help you to understand how you might compare to peers in your industry and what they feel you are ready and not ready for.

I must reiterate some of the cautions about codependence and guru-ism. Yes, the bulk of vocal education is transmitted in private lessons between a teacher and student, but sometimes, you can get too comfortable with a teacher. I have seen many singers and teachers approving of each other beautifully for years while glaring problems go unaddressed and progress dies. If you feel like you are going nowhere, you are probably correct.

Auditions, coaching, trusted friends' observations, voice lessons, and your own self-assessments should be consulted on a rotating basis. Sometimes, a change in one or more members of your team will give you fresh commentary and advice to act on. Or perhaps you just need a second or third opinion about something. Look for patterns. When you have a bunch of people telling you something similar, pay attention!

Perhaps you already have a great team, and outside opinions will just verify that for you. If you still feel that your progress is stagnating after making adjustments to your team, then consider the possibility that it is something *inside* you and not *around* you that needs to move. In that regard, do not hesitate to investigate counseling, life coaching, and soul-searching. These, too, are important parts of the artist's life. Everything relates to everything.

Feedback from the Arena

In addition to your team, you get clues about your progress from auditions, performances, competitions, and other people in your environment. Compared to your team, these are "less trusted others". Feedback from people who are not part of your team can range from helpful to useless. Generally, as with advice from your team, look for patterns that give you something to act on. Especially when you are young, many of the comments are conflicting, not just about your voice, but also about your talent, appearance, and career prospects.

Always consider the source. If the person giving feedback is someone you think is highly qualified, seek out another opinion and see if the average of the various comments starts to make sense as something you need to investigate. Singers, more than any other musicians, tend to get lots of comments from people who should mind their own business. Don't take anything too seriously until you gather as much evidence as possible from your team *and* the field.

Beware of the stranger who wants to talk to you about your "issues" and then tries to sell you a service to address them, especially right after a performance or audition. There are teachers, coaches, program directors, and others who may pitch a development opportunity to you that is mostly about a revenue opportunity for them. Take everything you encounter back to those in your inner circle of trust. Compare your team's ideas, the outside input, your own self-assessment, and your gut. In the end, you are always the boss of you.

If you are getting positive feedback about your singing, but *you* don't feel good about it, don't ignore yourself. I am a big fan of counseling in such a case so that you can deal with your self-critical thoughts appropriately. Life is too short to be unhappy with an activity that means so much to you. Sometimes, the problem is perfectionism. Sometimes, it's your knowledge that there is much potential you haven't reached yet. Sometimes, there might be a problem like depression, illness, or burnout that needs immediate attention.

The balance between how you feel about what you're doing and how others rate what you're doing is something all performers have to deal with. It's not easy, and it's always okay to ask for help. Take breaks! Have some time every day when you are not a singer. Take a week off once or twice a year with no practicing and no performing. It will help your mental balance immensely and help you to process comments and criticism better.

5. The Singer's Life

Practicing Better

What is practicing, really? Let's brainstorm. Practice is:

- exercise
- correcting weaknesses
- building strength and endurance
- concentrating on good form
- creating habits
- focusing attention on details
- learning a song
- figuring out what you want to express
- simulated performing

Practice success precedes performing success.

There are lots of good books available about how to practice. I'm not going to rewrite them. But one principle that will help every approach, technique, and tip is to *pay attention*. Repetition is a necessary part of practicing, but it doesn't have to be drudgery. If you learn to notice the many facets of the sounds you are making and the feelings you are perceiving, you will improve faster and enjoy it more. Developing a spirit of experimentation and curiosity to go along with the repetition is extremely helpful.

Drilling an exercise five times exactly the same way can send you into an automatic mode very quickly and possibly ingrain bad habits along with the good. However, if you vary each repetition in some small way, you will stay mentally focused and sing better generally. There is a strong chance you will discover new learning points on your own that you would miss with mindless repetition. To be a good learner of anything, but especially the singing art, we need to stay curious. The currently trendy word for this is "mindfulness".

What would smart, curious practicing look like? Let's say your teacher introduces an exercise to help you with your control of dynamics and registers, such as the one below. Here are some possible ways to practice this exercise to help you stay attentive, interested, and maximally productive:

Sing with /a/

- Start on random pitches rather than cranking up each repetition by half-steps.
- Add extra ornamental notes to any of the notes.
- Try all the flavors of the vowel and nearby vowels such as: /a/ ("ah"), /ɔ/ ("open O as in New York coffee"), and /ʌ/ "uh as in cup".
- Add accents to notes.
- Do it with portamento (sliding from note to note).
- Vary the tempo.
- Vary the dynamics on any of the notes. This will teach you a lot about why the pattern above was chosen in the first place.
- Change vowels when jumping the octave—notice how it feels different and coordinates the registers differently.
- Sing it with various meters (triple and duple).
- Play with the rhythm.
- Sing it backwards.
- Give it a mood—happy, tired, frightened, relaxed, jolly.
- Sing it with your body in different positions.

- Use words containing the vowels you are using, such as "Odd wands block all pawns" or "We three see green tea". Walter Foster's *Singing Redefined* (1998) has some wonderful phrases along these lines and gives many other inspirational ideas about mindful singing.

You can do these kinds of experiments with every exercise you work with. Such changes turn a bunch of exercises into a vocal behavior laboratory, where you pay attention and see what happens, and perhaps even begin to cause things to happen on purpose! You will go back to your teacher with a deeper understanding of what that exercise can do and perhaps open further dialogue about how to practice and what should come next. It makes you a participant rather than just a recipient.

Practicing and creativity belong together!

A New Voice Every Day

A person who has had to make a radical change in their thinking about an issue may begin to generalize that there are probably many other things they need to learn. This is the way of the inquisitive mindset. Being willing to have beliefs proven either true or false leads to a kind of openness that allows learning to accelerate. With experience comes the ability to absorb and process the new information in combination with what one has learned before—synthesis. Along with synthesis, one also learns when to reject ideas that are not useful.

As I wake up to my voice each day, I spend a few minutes playing with the attitude that I do not know my voice at all. How might I familiarize myself with a new voice, this voice that I have today, which might be different than ever before? As I get warmed up, and things seem to be possible or not, I usually recognize familiar patterns, sensations, and sounds. "Ah, this will probably be a Model 4QB day, although yesterday was more of a 7GV." If you always go for the 4QB every day because it's so darned good, what do you do when it just won't go there anymore? Do you keep trying to imitate yourself, or do you allow yourself to fully experience the essence of today's voice? Can you deal with finding a new vocal path if necessary, yet again? Are you willing to discover your voice every day?

When to Cancel

Sometimes you are just sub-optimal. It may be illness, a mood, life circumstances, lack of sleep, or a million other things. Singing on these days is sometimes discouraging. Yet sometimes, singing a little can cheer you up and turn a bad day into a good one. I encourage you to still do your gigs and lessons and coaching sessions and practicing when you feel a little "blah", because there will be times when you have to perform even though you aren't feeling perfect. Knowing that you can still achieve something on such days is a good thing.

However, it's also crucial to know where your "not today" boundary is. There is no gig worth hurting yourself for. There will be times where it's obvious that it isn't going to happen. Other times will be less obvious, and you will need to make a tough judgement call. Be honest and fair with yourself.

If you are unsure whether to cancel, get quiet and listen to your body and mind. Whether your bad day is seemingly all physical or has emotional causes, a quiet body will help you to find a quiet mind, where the best decisions come from. You cannot make the best decisions about anything from a place of anxiety, panic, or pressure.

Consistency

You may enjoy a great day, or string of days, in which you are singing very well. "This is so good! I am taking notes. This time I will remember what it feels like to sing well and I'll know what to do. I won't let this go." Then, you wake up the next day and it's gone. The easy resonance you had now feels like you're singing in an underground vacuum chamber. The high C that was so pure and strong has turned into a turbulent blob of shriekiness. The ease turns to drudgery. These are the familiar ups and downs of the practice room.

First, reason with yourself. If you got there before, you know it's possible. You will have better days.

Second, have a structure or set of principles you follow for checking in with your voice and making adjustments. That is, develop a system for dealing with today's voice, not the one you think you had yesterday or the ideal voice of the future. (Also see "Daily Technical Check-in" in Section 4.)

Third, look at how you're practicing when you're singing well versus when you are not. Sometimes when things are going great, we neglect practicing the things that got us there, and they may be things we need in our daily practice. Each singer has their own fundamental approaches and exercises that they need to keep up with for optimal results.

Sometimes self-assessments and self-corrections are enough to keep things humming along. Sometimes they are not. Don't be afraid to ask for help, whether from a voice teacher, a friend with excellent ears, or a medical professional.

At times, I have made myself crazy trying to capture breakthroughs and other good stuff in the practice room. I scribble notes, I record myself, I talk with a good singer friend. Over the years, I've found myself circling back to some concepts repeatedly. I have become friends with my issues, so I almost never throw a temper tantrum in the practice room anymore. I'm more likely to laugh at myself now.

It's amazing how one directive (either discovered or from a teacher) can feel completely different five years after the first time it was encountered. It can fail then and work now, or vice versa. I have to keep my mind open to accepting that anything or nothing could be true. Contradictions and paradoxes abound in our field.

Time, intelligent work, and patience bring consistency. This unmagical trio creates the magic.

Pre-Performance Performance

There are a lot of great books and workshops on how to prepare your material, which I will not have much to add to. However, I want to encourage you, at all stages of your career, to sing for small, friendly audiences before you take your singing into an audition, competition, or major concert. Sing for a group of supportive friends or family or at a nursing home or senior center. Singing for people who are inclined to love everything you have to offer is a great confidence builder and a very nice service to those people.

Going directly from practice room to high-stakes concert is a classically traumatic experience for younger singers. The degree recital, the finals of a competition, the important audition—can all bomb or succeed based on whether you have worked the kinks out in a less pressure-packed setting.

Points to ponder even before the try-out for a friendly audience:

In the practice room itself, it's good to practice performing a few times a week. Do a sing-through of whole pieces without stopping. Try singing to different targets in your practice room. Try it with eyes closed, visualizing a performing situation. Nit-picky practice of small sections of a piece can work out details, but run-throughs naturally feel very different and also need to be practiced. If you are doing a set of songs together in a performance, practicing in the order of the performance, without stopping, is essential to making it happen on the stage.

If you are preparing multiple pieces for an audition, practice them in every conceivable order, not just what you think the judges will ask for. It can be surprising how different they can feel when done "out of order".

Record yourself when you do these run-throughs. This kind of work will help you a lot at performance time. It is all too easy to have practice be one thing and performance an entirely different thing, which can make us much more uncomfortable than necessary when it matters the most.

Age

People are often concerned about the effects of age on the voice. This concern is certainly founded, as there are many examples of older singers having a less powerful voice than they did in their youth. However, advancing age does not mean that singers need to quit.

I received 201 complete responses from the Vocal Satisfaction Survey that I conducted in 2017. Many respondents in their 50s, 60s, and 70s felt that they were singing well, and most did not claim a decline in the previous five years. The most common issue associated with a decline at any age was a loss of range, almost always the high notes, but this was sometimes accompanied by new notes on the bottom. This bothered some, while other singers were philosophical about losing a few notes on top when other things were good.

In the survey results, I was struck by the lack of any clear trends about aging voices. Those who continued to sing and study were generally at least somewhat pleased with how they were singing. People who had retreated from singing and/or study had a less positive view of their current voices.

As a voice teacher who works with all ages, it is my experience that the main issue is good vocal exercise. If a singer stays active, sings repertoire that fits, and does not have terrible speaking habits, they can usually sing to an advanced age. I had a student who was in his mid 80s. His speaking voice had some of the typical markers of his age—breathy, crackly, lack of resonance, and frequent breaths. However, when he sang, his voice was much more clear and youthful sounding. He had a usable baritone range for his barbershop quartet and had a great time singing.

Nobody sounds exactly the same at 75 as they did at 25. This is not bad, it just is.

I attended a recital by Leontyne Price at the University of Iowa in 1982, around the time she retired from the opera stage. It was a little rougher vocally than we usually associate with her. I heard her again around 1986 at the University of Connecticut in a similar auditorium (about 2000 seats), and it was glorious. She sang well into her 80s. In interviews, she has talked about vocal care and continuing to practice. As a young woman, she overcame a vocal collapse and came back strong. She is a great of example of how conscientious care of one's own voice can keep one singing for a lifetime. I enjoy her frankness and charm when she talks about how she loves her voice.

Barbra Streisand's "Live at the Village Vanguard", recorded when she was 67, shows a voice with some fraying around the edges, less bombastic at the climaxes than in her youth, but what beautiful, expressive singing! Her other CD of that year, "Love Is the Answer" was Smooth Barbra, Mature Barbra. I have a friend who complained that Barbra isn't belting like she used to. So what?

We live in a noisy, loud, sonically abusive world. Much of our entertainment today is also noisy and harsh. A common definition of "good singing" often includes a "power" component that means "loud". Some are disappointed when a singer isn't loud like they used to be. Why?

A lot of singers realize that, at some point, they need to back off from applying force to the voice in order to stay healthy. This often means that they will be less loud. This is often seen as a sad thing. Ridiculous! Learning how to use the voice you have in a flexible and healthy manner is a fine choice. Often, it is the difference between continuing to sing or not.

Rosemary Clooney and Joni Mitchell kept lowering keys throughout their careers. Barbra is singing more gently. Tony Bennett finally sounds older at 90 plus! Magda Olivero made her sensational debut at the Met when she was 65! We are blessed to have had these singers in long careers, giving us mature interpretations that cannot be replicated by young people.

With age comes change, inevitably. As Joni Mitchell wrote in "Both Sides Now" — "something's lost, but something's gained in living every day". This may look like vocal decline to some, and indeed that may be a characteristic of many older voices. But maybe what we are hearing is something truer and wiser than what was possible when they were young. That is something to cherish. I love old singers!

Health

Body

Overall physical health will help your singing a lot. If you don't believe it, just wait until it leaves you sometime! You need to find out what healthy means to you. Fitness, body weight, flexibility, diet, hormonal regulation, and many other factors are highly individual. If you are coping with health issues and aren't sure where to start, I would suggest that you look for a medical team that has what is often called an "integrative" approach. Do some research on the terms "integrative medicine" and "functional medicine" and learn how they vary from other medical approaches.

The poles of exercise and rest are crucial. You need both. You don't have to run marathons and meditate for an hour daily, but you do have to have some deliberate activities for both exercise and relaxation. So many of us are sleep-deprived. Sleep is a good investment, not wasted time!

You can't deny the basic needs of food, sleep, exercise, and human interaction without risking health problems. It's beyond the scope of this book and my qualifications to get detailed in this section, so I will close by urging you to care for your body as well as you can. Your voice comes through your body. It doesn't take care of itself!

Soul

In her essay "What is a singer?", Camilla Strandberg gets to the heart of what, I feel, is a good principle for staying healthy as a human being who sings. It ends with "I will never 'be' a singer. I'll simply sing." (Strandberg, 2016).

145

It can be a trap to constantly call yourself a singer. To sum up your identity with one main label is dangerous. The "I" who claims a singular identity can get lost in it. You can wonder if you are worthy of the title when things get rough. If you lose your confidence, or you suffer a debilitating illness, or you have to tend to other things in your life, singing may take a back seat. Is there a threshold that you must stay above in order to keep the title "singer"? Do you have to be good enough or experienced enough or be able to impress others to keep the title? Do you have to prove to *yourself* constantly what it means to be a singer?

Does falling short of your vocal ideals change your identity? Not completely, if you are a human being first—a human being who sings. Singing is something you can do or not do. It can be a high priority. It might be your overriding passion, but it is not the whole of your being.

Social Identity

One social ritual I dislike is being asked the question "What do you do?". I sometimes answer "about what?" when I feel like being a stinker. I dislike the question because our culture is obsessed with work, and there are huge value judgements attached to it which I don't believe in. It's not always an easy question to answer if all or part of your career is in the arts. However, I realize that the inquirer is usually just trying to be friendly. How do you answer that question? If singing is a vital part of what you do each day, how do you mention it in combination (or not) with other parts of your doing self? Do you apologize for it, minimize it, maximize it, or mix it in equally somehow?

At this time, I tend to say something like, "I have a dual career in music and IT work. I teach singers in my private studio, do some performing and writing about music, and I work on databases

146

and websites." Nine times out of ten they ask a follow-up question about the music, not the technology, because it *is* more interesting. I can deal with whatever catches their fancy, but I want them to know that I do many things.

I know singers who don't talk about their "day jobs". In general, I now prefer to be an open book. Other people's possible judgements of my reality are no longer my concern, but when I was younger, admitting that I depended on non-music work felt like I was saying "I'm a failed musician". I'm so glad to be over that!

Retooling

Monica, a retired high school teacher in her 60s, came to my studio to see if she could get her voice to work better after years of decline. For the last few years of her teaching career, she had used a microphone to make herself heard in the classroom. A year of steady work with the right kinds of exercise brought out a beautiful soprano voice that allowed her to sing solos at her temple more confidently, as well as successfully auditioning for a community choir.

Rocker Eric, in his late 40s, came to me after a diagnosis of vocal nodules and his doctor's clearance to take singing lessons. His voice was breathy throughout, and his range and endurance were short. He wanted to continue writing and performing his songs as well as covers. Within a couple of years, he was doing much better and was able to sing over a two octave range with much more flexibility, ease, and power. He occasionally performs and finds that his songwriting has expanded with his voice.

Tina belonged to a huge church where she sang and played the trumpet. She came to me after her second vocal fold hemorrhage and decided to get some voice lessons for the first time in her life. She became able to make more sound with far less effort and force and learned the principle of making new behaviors into habits, while working with the natural responses of the body.

These singers were cleared by their throat doctors before coming to me. I am not a medical professional or speech therapist, and I am very careful to keep boundaries between teaching singing and practicing medicine. However, exercising the voice appropriately can yield great improvements and help to prevent new injuries. Sometimes these singers will sing even better than before because they know and use their voices better.

It can be difficult and demoralizing for a singer to realize that they either need to retrain and sing differently than before, or quit. Some people, like me, have traveled down "Retraining Road" multiple times. If you are in doubt about whether retooling is needed, track your voice in some kind of orderly way over time, such as using the SAPS (see Part 4), so that you have some perspective on your own singing.

If there have been any medical problems, or any are suspected, find an otolaryngologist who works with professional voices. It's useful to get a baseline laryngoscopic video and exam even if your voice is healthy. You can keep and compare the results with future exams as part of your overall lifelong vocal health process.

Retooling can be successful at any age. It's not uncommon to need to work through negative feelings such as shame, fear, exasperation, despair, and dread while one looks for answers and starts a recovery program. Persist. The human larynx and body are amazing and adaptable. Regardless of medical interventions or healing, proper use and exercise must be part of the long-term plan for your vocal future. Working with a good voice teacher will help.

Money

"When I argue with reality, I lose—but only 100% of the time."—
Byron Katie (Mitchell, p. 158)

Money is a sore subject for many people in the arts. Since my teen
years, many people have told me that the arts don't pay well, and
in general, that has been true for me. I don't have golden advice
here, but I want to tell my story, because I have made peace with
money, although it took quite a long time.

In Barbara Sher's *Refuse to Choose* (2006), the author coined the term
"Scanner" to refer to people who like to explore many interests.
She writes at great length about reconciling career and passions,
and I really resonate with her concept of the "Good Enough Job"
and feel that it is a great concept for good mental health.

"The best friend of almost every type of Scanner is what I call the
Good Enough Job. It isn't your dream job; it's the one that funds
your dreams. . . . Think of it: a job that doesn't bother you, whose
only crime is that it's just not enough to fulfill your life. But it
provides money and security and the freedom to fulfill your life in
your free hours." (Sher, p. 136)

After my bachelor's degree in performance, I was fairly certain
about two things. 1) I needed to make a living somehow. 2)
I wanted to go back for a master's while I was still young. I
became an office temp and was able to support myself between
my degrees. I was able to study and go places and take gigs
on the evenings and weekends, when virtually all the musical
employment happens, and not worry about having enough to eat.
I gained confidence in my ability to take care of myself by using
my office skills for income.

After my master's degree, in my late twenties, it was very important to me to try to "make a living with music". However, my graduate teaching assistantship had given me a disturbing peek into the politics of college teaching, which killed that career goal, and thus, I didn't feel inclined to go for a doctorate. Instead, I taught in public school for five years and hated it. I became ill, had nightmares, worked long hours, and was no better off financially than when I did office work. I'll never forget my relief and elation at giving my resignation to the school principal.

I had to go another way. I knew that I was capable of taking care of myself, which was a huge stress reliever. I went back to office temp work for a while. One long assignment gave me the opportunity to manage a small database, which became a new skill for the resume, and I was off and running on a technology track.

Ever since that time, I have made money with my increasing tech skills. During some periods, I have made more with private teaching than the tech, but most of the time, it has been the other way around. I used to feel embarrassed to admit this but no more. I have had tech jobs that offered great pay, flexible scheduling, and relatively calm atmospheres. I feel blessed. I have much respect for those who make a freelance career work, but I found it stressful because it killed my energy and dented my love for music. The scramble and hustle aren't for me.

In the big picture, the time spent at my Good Enough Job has been worth it. I am paid to keep increasing my tech skills, so that I can stay current and make a good living. I have the financial freedom to get all the lessons and coaching and educational experiences I need and to attend performances as well as create them. I get to choose my teaching clients and performance gigs carefully. I have time and perspective for writing. I am healthy.

Because I get paid for both teaching and performing, I am a "professional musician", but I don't limit myself to that. Even though there was a time when my revenue stream was "strictly music", I am happier now that that is not the case.

Many well-paying jobs in non-music fields are filled by good musicians. There are employers who like to hire people with music degrees for jobs requiring certain problem-solving skills, abstract thought, or logic. We musicians hone these skills with years of practicing our craft. The definitions of work and profession and career are all changing constantly in my world and probably also in yours, so stay open to the possibilities.

There is no shame in diverse revenue streams! Be your own patron!

Midlife and the Artist's Soul

There is a wonderful documentary film called *Best Worst Thing That Ever Could Have Happened*. Lonny Price directs the story of the 1981 Broadway premiere of Stephen Sondheim's *Merrily We Roll Along*. The show flopped and closed after 16 performances. The documentary uses film footage from the casting process and rehearsals of 1980 and 1981, along with many interviews with the cast, Stephen Sondheim, and Hal Prince. It is an interesting and moving film, especially for a performing artist.

The film struck a special chord in me because the people from that cast are my age. Hearing their stories about the excitement of being in a Sondheim show, most of them on Broadway for the first time, and then learning where they have gone since, was emotional.

When I was very young, I was enchanted by show business. I wanted to be an actor or a stand-up comic. As my teens went on, I focused on classical instrumental music. From my mid-teens until about 10 years later, my goal was to get at least one graduate degree in flute, an orchestra job, and a college or conservatory teaching appointment. Getting a professorship seemed like my professional pot of gold.

I received a reality check while working on my master's degree and teaching assistantship. I saw that academia was not quite as fabulous as I thought it was. There were many compromises and politics that disillusioned me. I am very thankful that I had that opportunity to learn more about college teaching before going for a doctorate.

During the second year of my master's I took an ethnomusicology course that made me aware of some of the many ways in which people outside of the Western classical tradition experience music.

I was suddenly perplexed about my allegiance to the conservatory model of musical education. Why did I think this was my path? What other possibilities were available? Why did I feel anxious all the time doing this "thing I love"? Did I really love it?

I described earlier in this book how I got back into singing by taking a break from the classical scene for a while. The hiatus helped me to find a good relationship with music again. Still, watching *Best Worst Thing* stirred up feelings about hope, inspiration, and aspirations that were upsetting. How much of what we accomplish is an unsatisfactory compromise compared to what we hoped for? Are dreams worth the trouble?

The actor Jason Alexander was cast in his first Broadway role in this production of *Merrily We Roll Along*, and he is featured in the documentary. Thirty years after his Broadway debut, he says that he often remembers the line from Pippin where a character says "I thought there would be more plumes." Jason talks about that line in relation to his career and the disappointments and disillusionments he has experienced.

Perhaps when we are young, we tend to think that everything will be amazing, perfect, and inspirational. Then with the years come challenges and failures, and our outlook changes. Most of us don't reach our youthful goals, and many of those who do are disappointed. It is virtually impossible and also practically unethical to tell a young person these things, so we must let them try.

Maybe if I had kept moving in a certain direction, not changing course so much, I would have achieved more. Maybe I would have had a higher professional status or higher-caliber performing experiences. Or maybe the best is yet to come. I know that at this age, I no longer judge people who haven't made it big. The definition of a successful life is very personal. Being a successful artist (which I can't even define anymore) isn't better than being a good teacher or mother or librarian or soldier. How stupid I was in my youth to think that these occupations could be judged and ranked!

It is harder than hell to keep going sometimes, but persistence seems to be a huge part of maturity's job description, so let's deal with it. Stagnation is certainly worse!

Regardless of your occupation, if you value love and beauty, and can add those things to the world a little or a lot, you are doing fine.

Action > Attitude

Everyone who has worked toward big goals over a long time has known multiple failures. I have not merely doubted my ability; I have judged it, fought it, cursed it, mocked it, and wanted to quit many times. That's just *self*-doubt, setting aside the garbage *other* people have thrown my way.

I have read a lot of self-help books about moving toward success. For the purposes of examining feelings of suckiness, they can be divided into two groups. In the first group are books with myriad strategies for how to develop and use a positive attitude in order to become more successful. In the second and much smaller group, we find strategies for moving on regardless of how crummy one feels. Rather than feeling like a failure at overcoming failure, I prefer the second group of books. It is has been encouraging to learn how to get moving again long before confidence comes (back).

Positive action is more important than a positive attitude!

Not waiting or expecting to feel happy and excited takes the pressure off waiting for a full recovery from failure. Why should we beat ourselves up for not having a perfect attitude? Doing one tiny, positive action each day has helped me and many other people through depression, writer's block, illness, self-doubt, self-sabotage, and other human darkness.

Write 50 words for your book. Do two push-ups. Fold a few towels. Answer an e-mail. Hug your kid. These small things will build your ability to get from "I suck" to "I can do stuff, whether I suck or not." Accomplishments and a positive attitude are both wonderful, but they don't always go together! A positive attitude without action is worthless, but a series of small actions will eventually add up to significant accomplishments, *regardless of your attitude*. It is a way up and out, no matter how bad, unfair, or inconvenient your circumstances have become.

Big Questions Again

There is much you can do for yourself after you have some training and experience under your belt. Along with being your own teacher more of the time, you can develop your ability to self-assess and to know when you need help. These skills, plus your interaction with the world, will help you to sort out much of the *what* and the *how* of your journey, but the following questions apply to every stage of your singing life:

- Why am I singing?
- What do I like to sing?
- Am I satisfied with my singing?
- What are my goals today?
- Have my goals changed over time?
- Am I getting closer to my goals? Why or why not?
- Am I growing?
- Am I performing enough or too much?
- Am I practicing enough and well? Why or why not?

These questions can be for you alone, or your team can help you, especially with the ones oriented toward goals. Make a note to yourself to revisit these questions at regular intervals, perhaps yearly. Regular journaling, such as that described in *The Artist's Way* (Cameron, 2016), can be very helpful.

In addition to the inwardly-directed questions above, you might also reflect specifically on your interactions with your team (teacher, coach, voice therapist, counselor, etc.) and your audiences:

- Is my teacher helping me to attain and maintain good vocal conditioning? What is the evidence for my "yes" or "no"?

- Am I getting sufficient coaching on my repertoire? Is my coach helping me to create better performances?
- Would another point of view on my strengths and weaknesses be helpful occasionally?
- Am I reaching the audiences I want to reach?
- How can I create performing opportunities?
- Do I have collaborators who I enjoy working with?

Openness

The concept of openness can be applied to every part of a singer's art and life. Open throat, open dialogue, open heart, open mind, open eyes, open communication, open to interpretation.

If you could suspend both belief and disbelief when presented with a new idea, what could you do with it? How might you examine it, play with it, experiment with it? What would happen if you waited 50% longer than usual to make up your mind?

How do those questions above feel if you substitute "supervisor", "work of art", or "technique" for the word "idea"?

What if it was not even possible to make up your mind about something really big? What if it just stayed open-ended, variably possible? Is it possible to live with a persistent "maybe"?

I change, therefore my singing changes. Since I don't know how I will change, I don't know how my singing will change. If those things are true, as they seem to be, then what I really need to have in place for my singing sanity are open attitudes, varied perspectives, and adaptable processes rather than rules and fixed identities.

I'm getting there. I have moments where I feel like I'm completely here, now. At those moments, openness is as natural as being.

Remember Fun?

All work and no play? Nope.

- Break into song at odd times when the urge hits.
- Entertain yourself in the shower and the car or when you are walking outdoors.
- Take singing breaks during your workday.
- Let a high note rip in an elevator or stairwell.
- Sing things that are outside of your usual repertoire.
- Sing with children and babies every chance you get.
- Sing to someone you love when you're feeling playful.
- Carry some karaoke backing tracks with you for parties. Karaoke nights out at a club can also be great fun.
- How would you sing for yourself if you loved your own voice? Make believe once in a while, if you don't love it yet.
- Don't be scared. Hardly anyone dies from singing anymore.

Love Yourself, Love Your Voice

Love for yourself must come before, apart from, during, and after singing. "Singer" is only one of the many things we are. It is vital for your mental and spiritual health to embrace all aspects of your humanity and not identify with being a singer only.

If you are kind to yourself and others, your singing will be lovely, even if unskilled. Our voices are tied so closely to how we express ourselves, and to how we feel, that it is difficult to become a truly different person when we sing. Like it or not, love for self and love for one's voice are connected.

Singing at its best can be a powerful expression of the gamut of human experience. Music and words can transport and transform. Great adventures await! By freeing your voice and singing music you love, you will realize your uniqueness and create joy.

Your voice is a miracle. Remind yourself often, however you can.

Peace on your way.

References

Dimon, T. (2011). *Your body, your voice*. Berkeley, CA: North
  Atlantic Books.

Garcia, M. (1847). *Traité de l'art du chant*. Paris, France: Author.

Husler, F., & Rodd-Marling, Y. (1965). *Singing: The physical nature of
  the vocal organ*. New York, NY: October House Inc.

Linking verb. (n.d.) In *Dictionary by Merriam-Webster: America's
  most-trusted online dictionary*. Retrieved from https://www.
  merriam-webster.com/dictionary/linking verb.

LoVetri, J. (2014). *Getting your voice together for the first time*.
  Retrieved from http://somaticvoicework.com/getting-your-
  voice-together-for-the-first-time/.

LoVetri, J. (2016). *Truth and paradox*. Retrieved from http://
  somaticvoicework.com/truth-and-paradox/.

Mitchell, B. K. (2002). *Loving what is: Four questions that can change
  your life*. New York, NY: Penguin Random House.

Reid, C. (1965). *The free voice*. New York, NY: Joseph Patelson
  Music House.

Reid, C. (2005). *Voice science: An evaluation*. Retrieved from http://
  corneliusreid.com/.

Sher, B. (2006). *Refuse to choose! : A revolutionary program for doing
  everything that you love*. New York, NY: Rodale.

Strandberg, C. (2016). What is a singer? [blog post]. Retrieved from
  https://www.camillastrandberg.com

Taylor, D. C. (1908). *The psychology of singing*. New York, NY: The MacMillan Company.

Tosi, P. (1743). *Observations on the florid song* (Galliard, J. E., Trans.). London, England: J. Wilcox.

Appendix

You may have noticed that this book, which is largely about training, does not actually contain much direct training material. Here in the Appendix I have included two exceptions. The essays "Potential in Every Note" and "Lamperti and the Evolution of Appoggio (Support!)" deal with two specific technical ideas that I feel are of crucial importance, but are not well enough understood today.

1. "Potential in Every Note" makes a plea for the use of the *messa di voce* exercise for all singers, regardless of voice type or genre. It was a foundational exercise in virtually all of the old European voice books, but is rarely used as such now. It has many benefits.

2. The ubiquitous word "support" must be addressed in detail. Francesco Lamperti was the first to define it, and based on his original words, it certainly didn't mean what people today say it means. This translation project was an eye-opener.

Potential in Every Note

The *messa di voce* is the act of beginning a single pitch softly, making a crescendo, then a diminuendo. It was considered important both as an expressive device and as a training tool in many Old School singing methods. It is found in the method books of Garcia, Marchesi, Crivelli, Mancini, Tosi, and the Lampertis, among others.

When a sung tone is poised in such a way that it can change volume, pitch, and vowel with ease, then it can be said to have maximal potential. It can go anywhere. With such potential, singing becomes a delight for both listener and singer. The voice sounds alive and vibrant, and is capable of vast expressive possibilities.

Whether the task at hand is a "wall of sound" passage from Wagner, Queen, or Jason Robert Brown, or something gentler, singing in such a way that the voice could at any moment break out into a cadenza or a series of *messa di voce* gestures keeps the voice happy and your options open. Singing with a multifaceted potential on every note ensures that the muscles will not be locked, breath pressure will not be excessive, stamina will be retained, vibrato will be available, and vowels will be recognizable. It allows the singer to express themselves more easily musically and dramatically.

How can one find this sort of potential on every sung tone? Practice! Functioning chest and head registers must be developed, then exercises that require fast movement, sustaining, and *messa di voce* dynamics—alone and in combination—are essential. There are myriad exercises that can be found or constructed for these elements. No single exercise or collection of exercises is the Holy Grail of training. The singer and the teacher, by using carefully honed listening skills, must determine what the voice needs. A way must be found to allow any tone to move pitch-wise, rhythmically, and/or dynamically without getting stuck in a position. Too many locked, pushed voices are not finding the ease which is every singer's right!

Much current vocal training does not adequately address how to build extensive dynamic potential. Dynamism is too often conceived of as something added to the voice, rather than being constantly available in every sung tone. There are traces of the idea of constant vocal potential in some singers and genres today, most notably in the more decorative renderings of some R&B and gospel singers. A healthy voice WANTS to break free now and then, and needs to be allowed to do so! The *messa di voce* can contribute to both agility and strength. Learning how to stay balanced without interfering tensions when moving between loud and soft singing helps pitch and agility as well.

In many of the old books, the 8 and 16 beat exercises that introduce the *messa di voce* can be daunting. However, there are great benefits to starting with much shorter notes and gradually extending them. A few minutes a day devoted to playing with the potential contained in a single note will rewarded with greater vocal versatility, guaranteed.

Lamperti and the Evolution of Appoggio (Support!)

The following article is a probe into the origins of the ubiquitous term "support". I have heard this term defined so many ways by so many people—some who sing well and others who sing poorly. When I looked at the Italian text where the term was first used, I was surprised to discover that it was quite different from the commonly used translation that is cited as "Lamperti". In my point of view, this is something of a scandal. Ideas of "low support" are often taught as being "several centuries old", but there is no evidence to back that up.

Francesco Lamperti (1811-1892) was a famous Italian voice teacher, as was his son, Giovanni Battista Lamperti (1839-1910). Francesco is one of the early sources of the word *appoggio* in voice teaching, which he first defined in his *Guida Teorico-Pratica-Elementare* (1864).

Appoggio has been a favorite subject in many books and articles up to the present day. It is translated as "support". "Support", in turn, has taken on a life of its own with many meanings and assumptions that go far beyond F. Lamperti's original definition. In the last century, "support" has become a quagmire. Ask five teachers what it means, and you will get at least five definitions, and many teachers will tell you that they avoid the word.

Lamperti himself changed his description of *appoggio* between his original publication of the *Guida* and his later published material. In 1876, Dr. Louis Mandl published a book titled *Hygiène de la Voix Parlée Ou Chantée: Suivie du Formulaire Pour le Traitement de la Voix* (Hygiene of the Voice Spoken or Sung: Followed by the Form of Treatment of the Voice). Dr. Mandl apparently had some influence over both Lampertis, as their writings after this time mention the

172

diaphragm and abdomen, which was not the case in Francesco's *Guida*. Previous Italian and French authors had mentioned very little about breathing and related body parts.

The *Guida* was revised and translated in 1890 into English as *The Art of Singing*. The title page contains the phrase "Revised Edition with Translation by J. C. Griffith". This edition has been widely cited in English writing about the voice. It contains a reference to Dr. Mandl and the influence he had on delineating abdominal, lateral, and clavicular respiration, among related concerns. Here we will look at Articles IV, VII, and XII. I will show how the 1890 edition differs from the 1864 edition, reflecting his evolving concept of *appoggio*, and concerns about breathing in general, in the late 19th century.

Articles IV and VII are in question-and-answer format. Article XII is written in regular paragraph style. The questions stayed mostly the same from 1864 to 1890, but the answers differed significantly, reflecting the trend to discuss the diaphragm, abdomen, and what has come to be called "breath management".

Below, for each of Lamperti's "Articles", I show: 1) the original Italian edition of 1864; 2) my translation of the original; and 3) the 1890 English edition.

Lamperti 1864:

ARTICOLO IV — DELLA RESPIRAZIONE

Cosa s'intende per respirazione?

S'intende la doppia azione dei polmoni di attrarre l'aria esterna e rimandarla con moto contrario.

* * *

My translation:

ARTICLE IV—ON RESPIRATION

What is meant by respiration?

It means the dual action of the lungs to draw in the external air and return it with contrary motion.

* * *

1890 English edition:

ARTICLE IV—ON RESPIRATION

What is meant by respiration?

It means the double action of the muscles of the thorax in receiving into and expelling air from the lungs.

The omission of the "action of the lungs" and the addition of "thorax" are interesting. Perhaps by 1890, Lamperti or his translator wished to be more inclusive about the role of the muscles of the torso in breathing.

In 1864, Lamperti does not give specific instructions about how a breath is to be taken. His anatomical references are limited to the lungs, which he explains are filled to different degrees depending on the phrase, while only the 1890 edition says later in the same Article that the breath is to be taken "first through the nose".

ARTICOLO VII—DELL'APPOGGIO DELLA VOCE

[FIRST QUESTION]:

Lamperti 1864:

Qual'è l'appoggio che devesi dare alla voce onde poter studiare senza stancare la gola?

È l'appoggio dei muscoli del petto e dell'aria concentrata nei polmoni.

* * *

My translation:

What is the support which should be given to the voice to be able to study without tiring the throat?

It is the support of the chest muscles and the concentrated air in the lungs.

* * *

1890 revision and translation:

What is the *appoggio* or support which should be given to the voice to enable one to study without fatigue to the throat?

The support afforded to the voice by the muscles of the chest, especially the diaphragm, acting upon the air contained in the lungs.

The 1890 version adds "especially the diaphragm", and omits "concentrated air". The use of "appoggio" in the translation indicates that the term may have started to be used in the English-speaking world.

[SECOND QUESTION:]

Lamperti 1864:

Come si ottiene tale appoggio del petto e del fiato?

Tenendosi nella posizione ed alle norme indicate all'articolo 3 ed aprendo bene il fondo della gola colla vocale *A* la voce sortirà limpida, sonora e bene appoggiata tanto nel piano che nel forte, cosa importantissima da ottenersi, dipendendo da ciò in buona parte l'esito della carriera. Dato il caso che l'allievo non potesse emetere la vocale *A*, bene appoggiata al petto e gli riescisse troppo aperta, o, como dicesi, nella maschera, oppure nasale, da principio potrà emetterla colla *L*, pronunciando *La*, onde facilitare il modo di renderla appoggiata e sicura.

* * *

My translation of the 1864 edition:

How is this support of the chest and breath obtained?

Holding oneself in the position and with the provisions contained in Article III and opening well the bottom of the throat with the vowel "*A*" will produce the clear voice, sonorous and well supported as much in piano as in forte, an important thing to be achieved, as on it will depend, to a large part, the success of the career. Given the case in which the student cannot emit the "*A*" vowel well supported in the chest, and it risks being too open, or, as it is said, in the mask or nasal, in the beginning he could emit it with "*L*", pronouncing "*La*", so as to facilitate the way of rendering it supported and secure.

* * *

1890 English edition:

How is this support to be obtained?

By observing the rules in Article III., with regard to position, and then opening the lower part of the throat with the vowel A. The sound thus produced will be clear and sympathetic; but if the pupil is not able to pronounce the vowel A with a full tone, let him first begin with LA, which will render its emission more easy and secure. This is a most important point for an artist to observe, as on it will depend, in the majority of cases, the success of his future career.

Here the opening question has been rewritten significantly. The words "breath" and "chest" are omitted. "Support" is the only noun left in the question.

In the answer, "with a full tone" replaces "well supported in the chest, and it risks being too open, or, as it is said, in the mask or nasal". Note that Lamperti considered "in the mask" to be undesirable in 1864, but had no such admonition in 1890. "Mask singing" became very fashionable in voice studios from Lamperti's time to the present day. The 1890 version also changes the location of the "as on it will depend, in the majority of cases, the success of his future career".

ARTICOLO XII:

Lamperti 1864:

APPLICAZIONE DELLA REGOLA PER L'APPOGGIO DELLA VOCE.

Per appoggio ossia regola del fiato s'intende che tutte le note dal basso all'alto e viceversa, sieno fatte col medesimo volume d'aria, trattenendo il respiro, cioè non permettendo che il fiato raccolto nei polmoni sfugga più del bisogno.

* * *

My translation:

APPLICATION OF THE RULE FOR THE APPOGGIO OF THE VOICE.

For support, namely, regulation of the breath, it is meant that all of the notes from bottom to top and vice versa, be made with the same volume of air, withholding the breath, that is, not allowing that the breath collected in the lungs escape more than needed.

* * *

1890 English edition:

THE APPLICATION OF THE RULE FOR THE APPOGGIO OF THE VOICE.

By singing *appoggiata*, is meant that all notes, from the lowest to the highest, are produced by a column of air over which the singer has perfect command, by holding back the breath, and not permitting more air than is absolutely necessary for the formation of the note to escape from the lungs.

1864 says that the notes should be made with the same "volume of air", while 1890 calls it a "column of air". The term "air column" is popular today in many voice and wind instrument studios. I don't know when it started, but Garcia and the old Italians did not use the term "columns". Also, "over which the singer has perfect command" and "for the formation of the note" were not in the original. It should also be noted here that Lamperti unambiguously says that support pertains to the regulation of the breath.

The Italian words for "abdomen", "abdominal", and any form of the word "diaphragm" do not exist in F. Lamperti's 1864 *Guida*. His son used the terms extensively in his 1905 book *The Technics of Bel Canto*, and was adamant that the chest NOT be involved in breathing, contrary to Francesco.

Can the typical voice teacher of today imagine "support" that is centered in the chest, and ignore the lower torso as F. Lamperti did in the *Guida*—indeed, as all those who came before him did? Why did he include a paragraph on the proper formation of the (Italian) /a/ vowel in a section dealing with "support"? What does the vowel and its origins in the body ("opening well the bottom part of the throat") have to do with "support"?

There are a lot of descriptions of behaviors labeled as *appoggio* today, most of them having to do with controlling skeletal muscles of the torso, but the *Guida* pulls in other factors, such as the way the vowel is made. I can see how Cornelius Reid and others believe that good singing creates its own feeling of "support". That is, good phonation has to develop first, and then the biofeedback of sensations of steadiness and security can start to be discovered. If there is nothing yet to support, then efforts to create support in isolation, as "preparation", make little sense.

The original *Guida* and the 1890 English version are in the public domain and freely available. Unfortunately, F. Lamperti's 1883 Italian title *L'arte del canto in ordine alle tradizioni classiche ed particolare esperienza* is difficult to find. If the 1890 edition is indeed an accurate translation of F. Lamperti's revised (1883) treatise, we see him in his later years pointing toward the modern idea of a complex system of "support". If the 1890 version is *not* a faithful translation, then we at least see how the editorial changes reflect ideas about "support" that had started to become popular in the late nineteenth century.

Authors Who Pushed Me

The books excerpted below have provoked me to ponder ideas that I might never have looked at if I had successfully gone through the voice-degree-music-school mill as a young man. I'm very thankful for the questions they raise, the solutions they propose, and the directions they have sent me as a singer-scholar.

Transformative Voice by Edward Foreman (1998) is one of the mind-openers that Justin Petersen brought to my attention. Some lines from the book that impressed me:

For those singers who are outraged at this attack on "beautiful tone," let it only be said that historically, the mania for beautiful tone is a recent deterioration in the art of vocalism. (p. 71)

Ultimately flexible and adaptable, the voice can work with very bad habits in place; but imagine how well it will work if we study and utilize its natural capabilities! Vocalism should be effortless; when it's not, the natural design and function have been ignored or violated. (p. 93)

The voice is an inseparable whole which — and here is a major paradox — must be worked with as though it were assembled from pieces. (p. 108)

One of Cornelius Reid's last major articles was *Voice Science: An Evaluation* which was rejected by the Journal of Singing, the official journal of the National Association of Teachers of Singing. They considered it too controversial. However, it was published in *Australian Voice* in 2005 (Reid 2005). Many of the writings of Reid could be included here. He was my very first "rebel author" in the field of voice pedagogy.

The decision to establish separate categories divided into trained and untrained singers for study and analysis, is apparently based on the mistaken assumption that trained singers have been well-trained and that untrained singers sing incorrectly. With respect to those who have been trained, it is evident that the findings are mainly of sociological value, since they have been based on current vocal fashions that are temporal, rather than an indication of a correct vocal technique. (p. 13)

One reason for the ready acceptance of "support" and the forcing of air as a pedagogic tool is that, with the exception of the diaphragm, the respiratory muscles are largely subject to volitional control, whereas the musculature responsible for vocal fold tension and laryngeal stabilization is not. Without a means for stimulating an involuntary muscular system, especially when there is an obvious need to institute some kind of control to facilitate the learning process, 'support' appears to offer a practical, if mechanistic, basis upon which vocal skills could be developed. (p. 14)

David Clark Taylor completed his substantial book (404 pages) *The Psychology of Singing* in 1917, but it is relevant to teaching voice today.

Like every other voluntary muscular operation, tone-production is subject to the psychological laws of control and guidance. Psychology is therefore of equal importance with anatomy and acoustics as an element of Vocal Science. (p. ix)

There is also another line along which all previous investigation of the voice is singularly incomplete. An immense fund of information about the vocal action is obtained by attentive listening to voices, and in no other way. Yet this important element in Vocal Science is almost completely neglected. (p. ix-x)

Herbert Witherspoon was an important American teacher who wrote the concise, wise, and good-humored *Singing: A Treatise for Teachers and Students*. I include here his excellent description of the problem of imagery and sensation as guides to better singing.

Sensation is responsible for much of the confusion in teaching, because teachers try to induce correct sensation in the pupil through imagination, imitation, or suggestion, in order to get the correct tone, instead of asking the pupil to 'do' something to cause correct action which produces correct tone, and which in turn will cause the correct sensation. That is, sensation is an effect and not a cause of tone. Correct sensation may be a guide after it has once been experienced by correct singing; it cannot be obtained except by correct singing. We may ask a man who has never eaten an olive what an olive tastes like, or what is the real 'taste sensation' of eating an olive. He will promptly voice his ignorance, and say, 'Let me eat an olive and I will tell you.' The sensation then becomes a guide for future eating." (Witherspoon, 1925, p. 38)

Your Body, Your Voice by Theodore Dimon (2011):

The notion, then, that in singing we create a supported column of air that involves greater pressure than during normal breathing is a fiction. (p. 46)

The larynx isn't a wind instrument—that is, it isn't meant to be vibrated by forcefully blowing air through the glottis. When working properly, the breathing and the larynx automatically work together so that the vocal folds vibrate very efficiently with an absolute minimum of air pressure. (p. 32)

Because abdominal activity is the most obvious aspect of muscular action that comes into play to produce sound, singers tend to latch onto this region as the focal point of vocal support. (p. 53)

Jeannette LoVetri is a highly respected voice teacher and trainer of teachers. I took several courses in her Somatic Voicework™ program, which I recommend. There is a unit in her coursework that deals with "pianoside manner", which emphasizes being student-centered, kind, calm, and respectful. She is a bold writer.

I'll close my section on influential authors with these inspiring excerpts from her blog, somaticvoicework.com:

If you teach and you accept everything a student does in a lesson — the good sounds, the not so good sounds, the attempts both failed and successful, the movements of the body and voice, the expression of the music, as if all of it were gifts, and if you treasure those gifts as they come to you, only good can come. (2014)

Coming home to the voice you have always had but didn't know you had is an extraordinary experience. Coming home to the voice you had to cultivate to take the place of the voice you had once upon a time is equally amazing. Either way, the journey is dynamic and challenging but rewarding. Finding a guide to help you along the way is a blessing. (2016)

Downloads

The complete *Self-Assessment Protocol for Singers* is available at sanesinging.com/saps.

On the web page above you will find:

- *Self-Assessment Protocol for Singers—Instructions.* This document contains all the tasks and instructions for administering your self-assessment.
- *SAPS Scoring and Comments.* This document is for compiling your scores and comments as you listen to the recordings you created with the SAPS.
- Links to sound files of the exercises used in the SAPS.

Recommended Reading and Media

Bloem-Hubatka, D.. (2012). *The old Italian school of singing: A theoretical and practical guide.* Jefferson, NC: McFarland & Company.

Brown, O. (1996). *Discover your voice: How to develop healthy voice habits.* San Diego, CA: Singular.

Cameron, J. (2016). *The artist's way: 25ᵗʰ anniversary edition.* New York, NY: Penguin Random House.

Clippinger, D. A. (1917). *The head voice and other problems.* Boston, MA: Oliver Ditson.

Edwards, M. *The college audition blog.* http:// auditioningforcollege.com.

Keeping, F. & Prada, R. (2005). *The voice and singing: Originally published in France 1886 as la voix et le chant traité practique par J. Faure.* New York, NY: VoxMentor.

Foreman, E. (1998). *Transformative voice.* Minneapolis, MN: Pro Musica Press.

Foster, W. (1998). *Singing redefined.* Fayetteville, AR: Recital Publications.

Harrison, P. T. (2014). *Singing: Personal and performance values in training.* London, UK: Dunedin Academic Press.

Harrison, P. T. (2006). *The human nature of the singing voice: Exploring a holistic basis for sound teaching and learning.* Edinburgh, UK: Dunedin Academic Press.

Kleon, A. (2012). *Steal like an artist*. New York, NY: Workman Publishing Company.

Lamperti, F. (1864). *Guida teorico-pratica-elementare per lo studio del canto*. Milan, Italy: Ricordi.

Mitchell, B. K. (2002). *Loving what is: Four questions that can change your life*. New York, NY: Penguin Random House.

Pressfield, S. (2012). *The war of art*. New York, NY: Black Irish Entertainment.

Reid, C. (1983). *A dictionary of vocal terminology: An analysis*. New York, NY: Joseph Patelson Music House.

Reid, C. (1992). *Essays on the nature of singing*. Fayetteville, AR: Recital Publications.

Rossini, G. (1827). *Gorgheggi e solfeggi*. Brussels, Belgium: L'Acadamie de Musique.

Sher, B. (2006). *Refuse to choose! : A revolutionary program for doing everything that you love*. New York, NY: Rodale.

Singer, Michael (2007). *The untethered soul: The journey beyond yourself*. Oakland, CA: New Harbinger Publications/Noetic Books.

Taylor, D. C. (1908). *The psychology of singing*. New York, NY: The MacMillan Company.

Tomatis, A. (2004). *The ear and the voice* (R. Prada, Trans.). Lanham, MD: Scarecrow Press.

Witherspoon, Herbert (1925). *Singing: A treatise for teachers and students*. New York, NY: G. Schirmer Inc.

Index

A
agility, 42, 118, 119, 123
appoggio, 17, 70, 73, 172

B
boundaries, 33, 35, 36, 137, 148

C
Christopher, David, 13
classical styles, 11, 13, 38, 41, 42, 48, 49, 52
Clippinger, David, 110
confusion, 80, 96, 183
contemporary Christian, 37
country, 37, 38, 41
Crivelli, Domenico, 170
cultivation vs. production, 17, 37, 92

D
degrees, 6, 7, 9

E
ego, 8, 23, 33
empirical approach, 11, 17, 79, 109, 110
exercises, 10, 11, 13, 15, 16, 29, 36, 47, 55, 56, 63, 64, 71, 104, 105, 124, 125, 135
expression, 10, 38, 42, 64, 83, 104, 118, 143, 162

T

talent, 6, 8, 40, 42
Taylor, David C., 17, 110, 182
teacher
  author's, 6, 10, 13, 14, 15
  finding, 28, 31
  role of, 26, 35
technique, 26, 41, 50, 55, 68, 70, 79, 91, 96, 133, 182
terminology, 37, 84
Tosi, Pier Francesco, 170

V

voice pedagogy, 28
voix mixte, 103
volume, 104, 109, 110, 123

W

Walkley, Mary, 10

About the Author

D. Brian Lee teaches singing at his studios in Potomac, Maryland and New York City. His clientele includes soloists, choristers, band members, Broadway and film actors, singer-songwriters, and voice teachers. In addition to his private studio work, his diverse career has included classroom teaching, leading master classes and workshops, and judging for competitions. He writes frequently about singing-related subjects at vocalability.com (http://vocalability.com). As a performer, his favorite repertoire is art song with English or Spanish texts, as well as chamber music.

Bachelor of Music, University of Iowa; Master of Music, Bowling Green State University; Bachelor of Science in Music Education, University of Maryland; Master of Arts in Instructional Design, University of Maryland Baltimore County.

CPSIA information can be obtained
at www.ICGtesting.com
Printed in the USA
FFOW03n0620060618
47075644-49469FF